White Rose MATHS

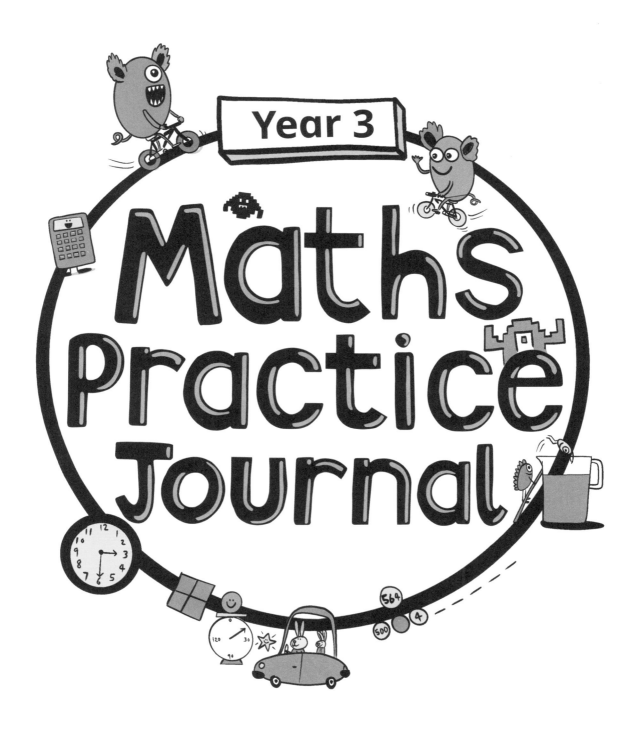

Year 3

Maths Practice Journal

Author: Caroline Hamilton

Series Editor: MK Connolly

OXFORD
UNIVERSITY PRESS

Contents

Autumn term
Block 1 Place value

 In this block, we explore **partitioning** numbers – that's when we break them down into smaller parts. Do you remember using **part-whole models**?

What's the missing number here?

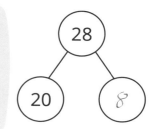

 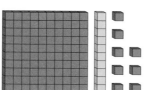 318

 We use **base 10** to help us. What's this number?

 We also use **place value charts**. They help us organise numbers into **hundreds**, **tens** and **ones**.

Here's one! Can you work out what number is shown?

Hundreds	Tens	Ones
100 100 100	10 10 10 10 10 10 10	1 1 1 1

364

We also use **number lines**. We label them and can use them to **estimate** where to put a number. Remember, "estimate" means to make a reasonable guess.

Can you estimate what number the arrow is pointing to?

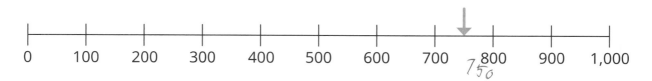

0   100   200   300   400   500   600   700   800   900   1,000

750

 Here are some maths words that you'll see. Can you remember what they mean?

ascending   descending   estimate   partition   more than/less than

order   compare   hundreds (100s)   tens (10s)   ones (1s)

Place value

Date:

Let's remember

1   How many sides does a square have?   4

2   How many minutes are in 1 hour?   60

3   What is 10 more than 20?   30

4   How many tens are there in 49?   4

Let's practise

1   Complete the sentences.

a)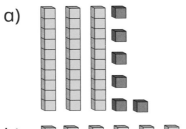

There are   3   tens and   6   ones.

The number is   36

b)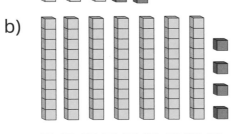

There are   7   tens and   4   ones.

The number is   74

c)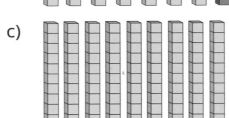

There are   9   tens and   0   ones.

The number is   90

2   Explain Tiny's mistake.

I have made 42

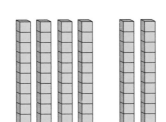

He put two tens insted of two ones

4

3   Complete the part-whole models and sentences.

a)
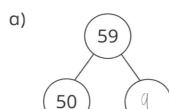

59 has [5] tens and [9] ones.

59 = [50] + [9]

b)
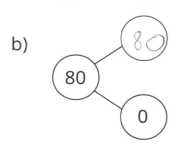

80 has [8] tens and [0] ones.

[80] = [80] + [0]

4   What numbers are the arrows pointing to?

Finding the halfway number first might help.

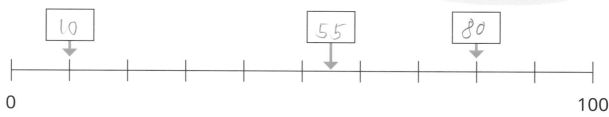

[10]   [55]   [80]

0   100

5   Complete this number line.

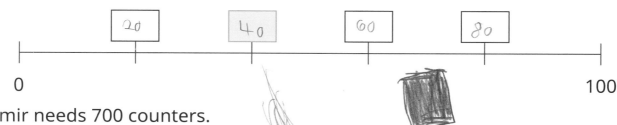

[20]   [40]   [60]   [80]

0   100

6   Amir needs 700 counters.

He has 400 counters.

Counters come in bags of 100

How many more bags of counters does Amir need? [3]

5

 **Talk it out**

Find out the age of everyone in your home or family.

Write each age using tens and ones.

Dora has done one for you.

Explain how you did this.

My gran is 76.
76 has 7 tens
and 6 ones.

How did you find these questions?

Place value

Date:

Let's remember

1 How many hundreds are in 400? `4`

2 43 has `4` tens and `3` ones.

3 How many hours are there in one day? `24`

4 Draw a circle around half of the counters.

Let's practise

1 What numbers are shown?

a)

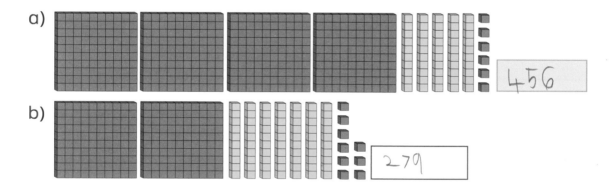

`456`

b)

`279`

2 Complete the sentences.

   a) 245 has `2` hundreds, `4` tens and `5` ones.

   b) 907 has `9` hundreds, `0` tens and `7` ones.

3 Complete the number sentences.

   a) 371 = 300 + 70 + `1`

   b) 198 = 100 + `90` + `8`

   c) 852 = `800` + `50` + `2`

7

4   Complete the part-whole models.

a)
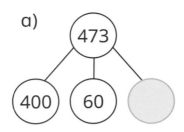

b)
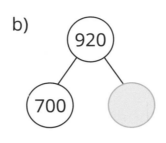

c)
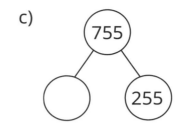

5   Complete the table.

For row 2, work back from 1,000 to find the starting number first.

100 less	10 less	1 less	Starting number	1 more	10 more	100 more
			260			
						1,000

6   Rosie has made a number using a combination of 5 of these counters.

Find 5 numbers she could have made.

_____

Q Crack the code

Use your answers in the coloured boxes to crack the code.

Can you use the code word in a sentence?

456	50	910	4	1	220	24	7	13
r	t	n	p	i	o	a	t	i

_____ _____ _____ _____ _____ _____ _____ _____ _____

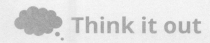 **Think it out**

Use part-whole models to partition 649 into 3 parts, in 6 different ways.

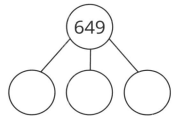

 Draw 5 more part-whole models like this.

 Talk it out

Teddy decides to add two more counters to the place value chart.

Hundreds	Tens	Ones
100 100 100 100		1

 The only new number I can make is 601

Is he correct? Explain your thinking.

 He is correct because …
He is incorrect because …

How did you find these questions?

9

Place value

Date:

Let's remember

1. What is 10 less than 302?

2. What is 100 + 100 + 100 + 10 + 4?

3. Circle $\frac{1}{3}$ of the counters.

4. What is 35 ÷ 5?

Let's practise

1. Complete each number line.

   a)

   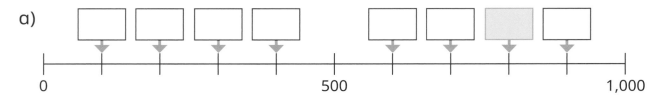

   b)

   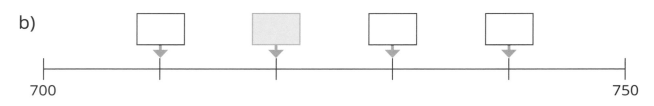

   c)

   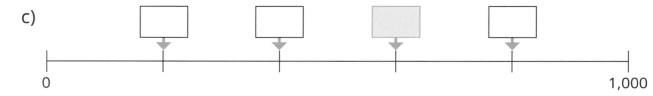

2. Tiny thinks the arrow is pointing to 610

   Explain why Tiny is wrong.

   _____

   _____

3   a) Estimate the number the arrow is pointing to on the number line.

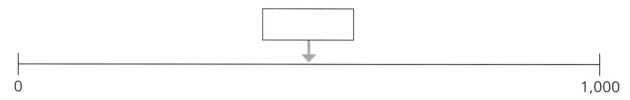

0   1,000

To estimate, make a
reasonable guess.

b) Draw an arrow to estimate where 200 is on the number line.

4   Circle all the numbers that are greater than 712

699   900   713   711   721

Write the numbers you circled from greatest to smallest.

_____

5   Fill in the missing digit to make the statement correct.

317 > 3 ☐ 7

6   The 3-digit numbers are in ascending order.

☐47, 213, 2☐9, ☐31, 300

Work out the missing digits.

Remember, "ascending order"
means from smallest to greatest.

Crack the code

Use your answers in the coloured boxes to crack
the code.

0	2	7	720	1	292	800	600
v	l	n	e	a	i	t	r

Can you explain what
the code word means to
someone at home?

_____ _____ _____ _____ _____ _____ _____ _____

Real world maths

Make your own number lines using string, pegs and paper.

Hide some of the numbers from your number line.

Ask someone at home which numbers you have hidden.

Now can you make a different number line? And another?

 ## Talk it out

Ask someone at home to play with you.

Roll a dice 3 times to make a 3-digit number.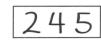

Do this twice more until you have three different 3-digit numbers.

Write your numbers in ascending order.

Explain how you ordered them.

 First, I looked at the digit in the ... place. Then I ...

Make three more 3-digit numbers.

Put all six numbers in descending order. Explain how you ordered them.

How did you find these questions?

Block 2   Addition and subtraction

In this block, we explore addition and subtraction.

We use **number bonds** to help. In these **part-whole models**, the missing **wholes** are numbers 5 and 50

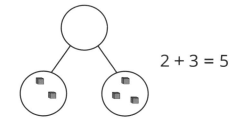

$2 + 3 = 5$

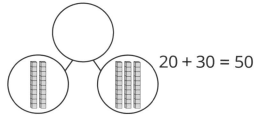

$20 + 30 = 50$

We **partition** numbers and use **number lines** to help us add and subtract.

The first number line shows $350 + 80$

The second shows $244 - 7$

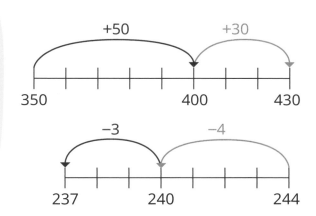

Hundreds	Tens	Ones

Place value charts help us complete column additions.

$345 + 432$ can be represented like this.

We use **bar models** to represent problems and to show **fact families**.

82	
39	43

Here are some maths words that you'll see. Can you remember what they mean?

whole   part   add   subtract   plus   minus

multiply   number bond   more   less   fact family   complement

Addition and subtraction

Date:

Let's remember

1 Complete the number track. | 50 | 100 | 150 | | | | |

2 What is 100 less than 520?

3 738 = 700 + ⬚ + 8

4 Write the time the clock shows in words.

_____

Let's practise

1 Complete the calculations.

a) 4 + 3 = ⬚

40 + 30 = ⬚

400 + 300 = ⬚

b) 9 – 1 = ⬚

90 – 10 = ⬚

900 – 100 = ⬚

2 a) Here is a number.

H	T	O
100 100	10 10	1 1
100 100		1
100 100		

Add 5 ones to the number.
What is the number now?
⬚

b) Here is a number.

H	T	O
100 100	10 10	1
100	10 10	
	10	

Add 4 tens to the number.
What is the number now?
⬚

14

3 Complete the number sentences.

a) 326 + 30 = ☐

c) 989 − 50 = ☐

b) 852 + ☐ = 892

d) 763 − ☐ = 703

4 Tiny adds 3 tens to 762

Tiny's answer is 765

Explain the mistake Tiny has made.

_____

5 Complete the part-whole models.

a)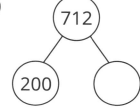

b)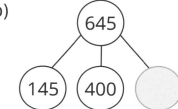

6 Annie is selling cakes at the weekend.

She has 175 cakes and bakes 300 more.

On Saturday, she sells 200 cakes.

On Sunday, she eats 1 cake and sells 200 cakes.

How many cakes does Annie have left?

🔍 **Crack the code**

Use your answers in the coloured boxes to crack the code.

391	60	30	74	800	100	356	70
d	e	h	s	n	d	r	u

Can you use the code word in a sentence?

____ ____ ____ ____ ____ ____ ____ ____

15

 **Think it out**

Use paper or card to make counters.

You will need to make ten of each type of counter.

H	T	O

Now start making numbers!

Make 896

Subtract 7 hundreds.

What number do you have now?

You could use a 5 pence coin as a counter template.

Make up some questions of your own for someone else to try!
Check their answers.

 Talk it out

Work out the values of the missing digit cards.

| 4 | | 6 | + | 7 | | = | | 9 | 6 |

Explain to someone how you worked out the value of each card.

 I started by …
That helped me work out the value of the …

How did you find these questions?

Addition and subtraction

Date:

Let's remember

1 753 – 20 = ▢

2 500 + 300 = ▢

3 647 = 500 + ▢ + 7

4 Shade $\frac{1}{3}$ of the shape.

Let's practise

1 Use the number lines to help you work out the additions.

a) 146 + 7 = ▢

b) 309 + 5 = ▢

2 Tiny has worked out 132 – 9 by counting back in 1s.

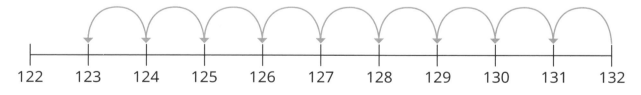

Draw a number line to show how Tiny could work out 132 – 9 in a more efficient way.

"Efficient" means quick or simple.

3 Work out the subtractions.

a) 641 – 4 = [ ]

| | | | | | | | | | | |
|631|632|633|634|635|636|637|638|639|640|641|

b) 363 – 7 = [ ]   c) 555 – 8 = [ ]

4 Complete the additions.

270 + 10 = [ ]   270 + 30 = [ ]

270 + 20 = [ ]   270 + 40 = [ ]

Can you spot a pattern?

5 Complete the calculations.

a) 230 – 40 = [ ]   c) 604 – [ ] = 554

b) 725 – 30 = [ ]   d) 147 – [ ] = 87

6 Write the missing digits.

[ ]28 – [ ]0 = 478

🔍 Crack the code

Use your answers in the coloured boxes to crack the code.

695	290	140	733	637	60	314	547
c	a	u	s	t	t	b	r

Can you use the code word in a sentence?

_____ _____ _____ _____ _____ _____ _____ _____

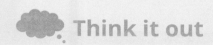 **Think it out**

Roll a dice 4 times to get 4 digits.

Arrange your digits to make 4 different subtractions.

☐ ☐ ☐ – ☐ 0

Work out the answer to each of your calculations.

☐ – ☐ = ☐   ☐ – ☐ = ☐

☐ – ☐ = ☐   ☐ – ☐ = ☐

 Talk it out

Work out 203 – 9 in 3 different ways.

Show your working for each method.

Explain why each method works.

 This method works because …

How did you find these questions?

Addition and subtraction

Date:

Let's remember

1   630 – 70 = ☐

2   745 – ☐ = 345

3   365 = 300 + ☐ + ☐

4   10 g + 10 g + 10 g + 2 g + 2 g + 2 g = ☐ g

Let's practise

1   Complete the sentences.

a) There are ☐ ones in 10

b) There are ☐ tens in 100

2   a) How many ones are in 3 tens? ☐

b) How many tens are in 5 hundreds? ☐

c) How many hundreds are in 40 tens? ☐

3   Complete the column addition.
Use the place value counters to help you.

Hundreds	Tens	Ones
100 100 100 100	10 10 10 10 10	1 1 1
+ 100 100		1 1 1 1

	H	T	0
	4	5	3
+	2	0	4

4 Complete the column additions.

a)

	H	T	O
	3	7	7
+	3	2	1

b)

	H	T	O
	6	0	4
+	2	9	0

5 Complete the subtraction.
Cross out counters in the place value chart to show your working.

Hundreds	Tens	Ones
100 100 100	10 10	1 1 1 1 1 1

	H	T	O
	3	2	6
−	1	2	5

6 Complete the subtractions.

a)

	H	T	O
	8	4	7
−	5	0	3

b)

	H	T	O
	9	5	1
−	2	4	0

7 Find two odd numbers that add together to make 758

[   ] + [   ] = 758

Q Crack the code

Use your answers in the coloured boxes to crack the code.

4	201	711	50	400	698	344	10
h	n	e	c	e	a	g	x

Explain what the code word means to someone.

____ _____ _____ _____ _____ _____ _____ _____

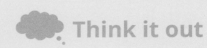 Think it out

Work out the value of each shape.

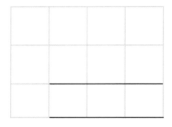

★ = ☐   ▲ = ☐   ● = ☐

Create your own shape calculation using three different shapes.

 Talk it out

Work out 354 – 244 using the column method.

Think of some other methods you could use to solve this subtraction.

Explain each of your methods to someone.

Which method do you prefer? Why?

I prefer this method because …

How did you find these questions?

Addition and subtraction

Date:

Let's remember

1 875 – 442 = ⬚

2 What is the missing digit?

$26\boxed{} - 3 = 265$

3 Circle all the numbers that are greater than 450

800   496   399   452   267   442   500

4 27 + 46 = ⬚

Let's practise

1 Tiny has completed this addition.

		3	4	5
+		1	2	5
		4	6	10

What mistake has Tiny made?

_____

Work out the correct answer.

		3	4	5
+		1	2	5

2 Complete the additions.

a)

		5	3	6
+		2	2	5

c)

		9	5	8
+			6	7

b)

		7	4	4
+		1	3	9

d)

		1	1	6
+		7	9	4

3   Tiny works out 853 – 215 and gets the answer 642

What mistake has Tiny made?

_____

_____

4   Work out the subtractions.

a)
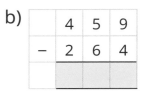

	7	4	6
−	5	2	7

b)
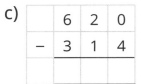

	4	5	9
−	2	6	4

c)
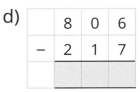

	6	2	0
−	3	1	4

d)

	8	0	6
−	2	1	7

5   Complete the calculations.

a) 97 + 483
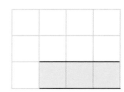

b) 703 – 251

Think about how to line up your digits.

6   Mo runs 207 m.

Whitney runs 319 m further than Mo.

How many metres do Whitney and Mo run altogether? [   ] m

🔍 Crack the code

Use your answers in the coloured boxes to crack the code.

910	580	761	195	433	589
l	n	o	u	c	m

Can you use the code word in a sentence?

_____ _____ _____ _____ _____ _____

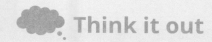 **Think it out**

Write an addition with ones that total more than 10 (like 26 + 15 = 41)

Write an addition with tens that total more than 100 (like 45 + 83 = 128)

Write a worded question for each of your additions.

 Talk it out

Each of these calculations has a mistake.

	2	1	5
+		3	7
	5	**8**	**5**

	8	0	7
−	3	5	2
	5	**5**	**5**

	4	6	7
−	1	9	2
	6	**5**	**9**

Explain each mistake to someone in your home.

 In this calculation, the mistake is …
I knew it was a mistake because …

Work out the correct answers.

How did you find these questions?

25

Addition and subtraction

Date:

Let's remember

1   786 – 59 = ☐

2   What is 274 more than 351? ☐

3   400 + ☐ = 900

4   How many minutes are there in half an hour? ☐

Let's practise

1   Here is a hundred square.

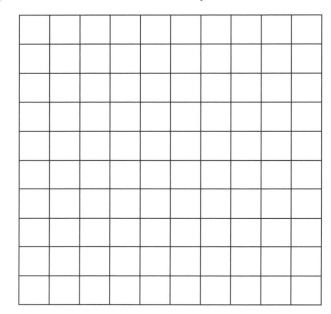

a) Shade 33 squares.

b) What is the complement of 33 to 100? ☐

c) Complete the number sentence.

33 + ☐ = 100

2   Tiny has filled in the missing digit in each calculation.

| 25 + 7 **5** | 49 + **5** 1 | 35 + 6 **5** | 53 + **5** 7 |

Is Tiny correct? _____

These all show complements to 100

Explain your answer.

_____

26

3 Find the complements to 100

a) ☐ + 64 = 100

b) ☐ + 8 = 100

c) 100 = 19 + ☐

d) 100 = ☐ + 55

4 a) Complete the sentences to estimate the answer to 787 + 95

787 is close to ☐

95 is close to ☐

My estimate is ☐

b) Estimate the answer to 398 – 206 ☐

5 A school has 300 cakes to sell to raise money for charity.

- Teachers buy 103 cakes.
- Children buy 96 cakes.
- Visitors buy 49 cakes.

a) Estimate how many cakes the school has left to sell. ☐

b) Work out the exact number of cakes the school has left to sell. ☐

Crack the code

Use your answers in the coloured boxes to crack the code.

67	52	625	81	30	36
m	r	n	e	u	b

Can you give someone an example of the code word?

_____ _____ _____ _____ _____ _____

27

Talk it out

Play "Complements to 100" with someone in your home.

Close your eyes and point to a number on the hundred square. Open your eyes and call out the number.

The other player calls out the complement to 100

Check they are correct.

Swap roles and play again.

1	2	3	4	5	6	7	8	9	10
11	12	13	14	15	16	17	18	19	20
21	22	23	24	25	26	27	28	29	30
31	32	33	34	35	36	37	38	39	40
41	42	43	44	45	46	47	48	49	50
51	52	53	54	55	56	57	58	59	60
61	62	63	64	65	66	67	68	69	70
71	72	73	74	75	76	77	78	79	80
81	82	83	84	85	86	87	88	89	90
91	92	93	94	95	96	97	98	99	100

 I know that is the complement to 100 because …

 Real world maths

Choose a short physical activity you enjoy doing.

Now estimate how many you could do in 1 minute.

Ask someone at home to estimate too.

I will do star jumps!

Now do your activity. Ask someone to time you and count how many.

Whose estimate was closer?

How did you find these questions?

Block 3 Multiplication and division A

In this block, we explore **multiplication**, which is the **repeated addition** of groups of **equal sizes**.

Here are 3 equal groups with 2 in each group. 3 × 2 = 6

We also explore **division**, which is sharing into equal groups or grouping into groups of a certain number.

6 ÷ 2 = 3

6 ÷ 3 = 2

We use **arrays** to show the link between repeated addition and multiplication.

This array shows 3 + 3 + 3 + 3 = 12 and also 3 × 4 =12

We use **bar models** to help with **sharing** and **grouping** problems.

The first bar model shows 20 sweets shared equally between 5 friends. The second bar model shows 20 sweets grouped into bags of 5

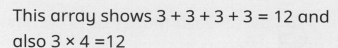

Here are some maths words that you'll see. Can you remember what they mean?

multiply   divide   times   sharing   grouping   equal parts

arrays   commutative   column   row   repeated addition   multiple

Multiplication and division A

Date:

Let's remember

1. 203 – 156 = ☐

2. What is 546 minus 53? ☐

3. Find the difference between 311 and 10 ☐

4. Complete the number track.

$\frac{0}{4}$	$\frac{1}{4}$	$\frac{2}{4}$		

Let's practise

1. Complete the sentences to describe the groups.

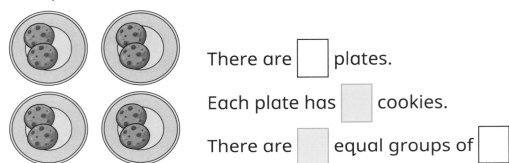

There are ☐ plates.

Each plate has ☐ cookies.

There are ☐ equal groups of ☐

2. Draw a picture to show these groups:

   • There are 5 plates.

   • Each plate has 3 apples.

   • There are 5 equal groups of 3 apples.

3. Here is an array.

   a) How many rows are there? ☐

   b) How many columns are there? ☐

   c) Complete the multiplication for the array. ☐ × ☐ = ☐

4   Use the bar models to complete the divisions.

a) 35 ÷ 5 = ☐

b) 60 ÷ 10 = ☐

5   Use the array to complete the calculations.

a) 2 × 4 = ☐

b) 8 ÷ 2 = ☐

6   Tick the statements that are true.

All multiples of 10 end in 0	All multiples of 5 end in 5	All multiples of 2 end in 2
☐	☐	☐

A multiple is made by multiplying two whole numbers greater than 1

Crack the code

Use your answers in the coloured boxes to crack the code.

6	3	4	301	12	2	7
l	q	e	u	u	n	a

What word is the opposite of the code word?

____ ____ ____ ____ ____ ____ ____

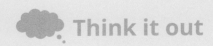 **Think it out**

Roll a dice three times to make a 3-digit number.

Write the number.

     315

Do this 9 more times until you have 10 numbers.

For each number, ask:

- Is it a multiple of 2?
- Is it a multiple of 5?
- Is it a multiple of 10?

If it is a multiple, record this in the tally chart.

Multiple	Tally
Multiple of 2	
Multiple of 5	
Multiple of 10	

Which was the most likely multiple? Why?

Is it possible to roll a multiple of 10? Why or why not?

Share what you find out with someone in your home.

How did you find these questions?   ☹

Multiplication and division A

Date:

Let's remember

1 What is 40 divided by 5?

2 Estimate the answer to 398 + 48

3 Write the numbers in order starting with the smallest.

505   510   499   501

_____

4 How many vertices does a triangle have?

Let's practise

1 Complete the sentences.

There are ☐ equal groups of ☐

☐ × ☐ = ☐

☐ + ☐ + ☐ + ☐ + ☐ + ☐ = ☐

2 Tiny is circling groups of 3

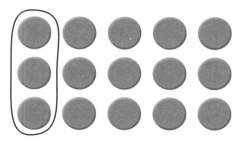

a) Complete Tiny's drawing so that all groups of 3 are circled.

b) How many groups of 3 are there?

c) How many counters are there in total?

d) What is 15 ÷ 3?

33

3   Write two multiplication and two division facts shown by the array.

☐ × ☐ = ☐   ☐ ÷ ☐ = ☐

☐ × ☐ = ☐   ☐ ÷ ☐ = ☐

4   Complete each bar model.

a)
24		
8	8	

c)
18		

b)
9	9	9

d)
33		

5   Complete the number sentences.

a) $3 \times 2 = $ ☐   c) $3 = 3 \times$ ☐   e) ☐ $= 12 \times 3$

b) $0 \times 3 = $ ☐   d) $3 \times 6 = $ ☐   f) $7 = $ ☐ $\div 3$

6   Eva gets £3 pocket money each week.

She wants to buy a game that costs £28

How many weeks' pocket money does Eva need to buy

the game? ☐

Real world maths

Get spotting!

How many things can you spot at home or outside that are in groups of 3?

I'm trying to spot flowers in groups of 3.

Count in 3s to find how many there are altogether of each of the things you spot.

Draw some of them here.

 Talk it out

1	2	3	4	5	6	7	8	9	10
11	12	13	14	15	16	17	18	19	20
21	22	23	24	25	26	27	28	29	30
31	32	33	34	35	36	37	38	39	40
41	42	43	44	45	46	47	48	49	50

Shade all the numbers in the 3 times-table.

One has been done for you.

Talk about any patterns that you can see.

 The pattern I can see is ...

How did you find these questions?

35

Multiplication and division A

Date:

Let's remember

1 What is 7 × 3?

2 Write three multiples of 5

3 45 + ☐ = 100

4 What is half of 8?

Let's practise

1 Tiny is making an array to show the multiplication 6 × 4

a) Draw more counters to complete Tiny's array.

b) How many rows are there in the completed array?

c) How many columns are there in the completed array?

d) How many counters are there in total in the completed array?

2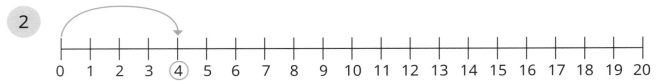

a) Use the number line to show jumps of 4 to 20
    The first jump has been done for you.

b) How many jumps did you draw in total?

c) Use the number line to complete the calculations.

1 × 4 = ☐   3 × 4 = ☐   5 × 4 = ☐

2 × 4 = ☐   4 × 4 = ☐

3   Teddy has made this array.

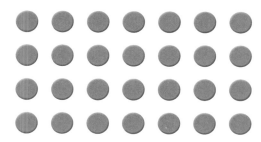

   a) How many groups of 4 are there? ☐

   b) Complete the division 28 ÷ 4 = ☐

4   Complete the number sentences.

   a) 4 × 2 = ☐   c) 0 × 4 = ☐

   b) ☐ = 12 × 4   d) 9 = ☐ ÷ 4

5   Write <, > or = to compare the statements.

   a) 3 × 7 ◯ 4 × 7   c) 0 × 4 ◯ 0 × 3

   b) 3 × 4 ◯ 4 × 3   d) 3 × 10 ◯ 30 ÷ 10

6   Mrs Smith buys 9 packs of pencils and 6 packs
     of glue sticks.

     How much money does Mrs Smith spend in total?

     £ ☐

Q **Crack the code**

Use your answers in the coloured boxes to crack the code.

16	6	55	24	21	7	48	5
a	t	s	i	e	t	e	m

Can you explain
the code word
to someone?

____ ____ ____ ____ ____ ____ ____ ____

 **Talk it out**

List the 2, 3, 4, 5 and 10 times-tables up to 12 × on a separate sheet of paper.

Do any of the times-tables have all even numbers?

Do you notice any patterns between the times-tables?

Do any of them have all odd numbers? Why do you think this is?

Share your thinking with someone in your home.

 The patterns I've spotted are …

 Real world maths

Find out the age of as many people as you can.

Are any of their ages a multiple of 2, 3, 4, 5 or 10?

_____

How do you know?

_____

When will your age next be a multiple of 2, 3, 4, 5 or 10?

_____

How did you find these questions?

Multiplication and division A

Date:

Let's remember

1. ☐ × 4 = 44

2. What is 27 divided by 3? ☐

3. What addition could you do to check that 481 – 55 = 426? _____

4. Write <, > or = to compare the lengths.

    32 m ◯ 32 cm

Let's practise

1. Write the multiplication that each image shows.

    a)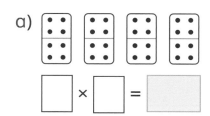

    ☐ × ☐ = ☐

    b)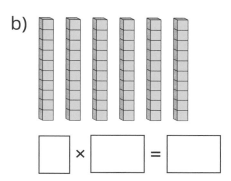

    ☐ × ☐ = ☐

2. 24 grapes are shared between 3 plates.

    Complete the sentences.

    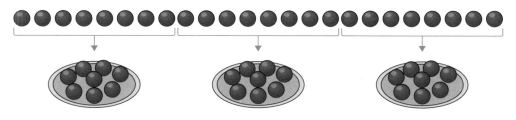

    There are ☐ grapes on each plate.

    There are ☐ plates.

    24 shared into ☐ equal groups is ☐

39

3 What divisions are shown on the bar models?

Complete the bar models and number sentences.

a)

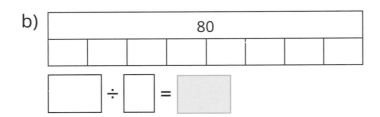

8

☐ ÷ ☐ = ☐

b)

80

☐ ÷ ☐ = ☐

4 Complete the calculations.

a) 8 × 2 = ☐

b) 8 × 6 = ☐

c) 0 × 8 = ☐

d) ☐ = 12 × 8

e) 8 = 8 × ☐

f) 7 = ☐ ÷ 8

5 Use the fact 3 × 8 = 24 to work out 30 × 8 ☐

6 Ron is in a shed clearing it out.

In the shed, Ron spots 12 spiders. Each spider has 8 legs.

How many legs are there in the shed in total? ☐

🔍 Crack the code

Use your answers in the coloured boxes to crack the code.

3	56	9	10	48	32	8
m	e	c	a	r	o	p

Can you use the code word in a sentence?

_____ _____ _____ _____ _____ _____ _____

Talk it out

On the hundred square:

- shade the 2 times-table.

- circle the 4 times-table.

- cross out the 8 times-table.

Tell someone what you notice.

 I notice that …

1	2	3	4	5	6	7	8	9	10
11	12	13	14	15	16	17	18	19	20
21	22	23	24	25	26	27	28	29	30
31	32	33	34	35	36	37	38	39	40
41	42	43	44	45	46	47	48	49	50
51	52	53	54	55	56	57	58	59	60
61	62	63	64	65	66	67	68	69	70
71	72	73	74	75	76	77	78	79	80
81	82	83	84	85	86	87	88	89	90
91	92	93	94	95	96	97	98	99	100

 Think it out

Eva, Dora and Mo are working out 14×8

 I am going to multiply 14 by 4, then double the answer.

 I am going to double 14, then double the answer and then double it again.

 I am going to multiply 14 by 10 then subtract double 14

Work out 14×8 using each method.

Which method do you prefer, and why?

_____

_____

How did you find these questions?

Time to reflect

Look back through the work you have done this term.
Think about what you enjoyed and what you found easy or hard.
Talk about this to your teacher or someone at home.

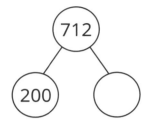

Look back at the part-whole models on page 5.
What's the missing part here?
How did you find this? Circle one of the statements.

1	2	3	4
I found this hard and need some help.	I need some more practice.	I can do this well and didn't make any mistakes.	I am confident and could teach someone else.

Go to pages 20–21.
Look at your column additions and subtractions. Can you complete these questions?

	H	T	O
	4	5	3
+	2	0	4

	H	T	O
	6	4	5
–	2	3	1

How did you find them?
Circle one of the statements to show how you feel.

I am confident and could teach someone else.	I think I understand but I need more practice.	I don't understand and need help.

Look back at the multiplications and divisions in Block 3.
Can you complete these?

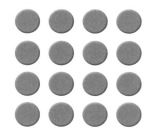

	16		
4	4	4	4

$\boxed{} \times \boxed{} = \boxed{}$ $\boxed{} \div \boxed{} = \boxed{}$

How did you find this?
Colour in one of the faces to show how it made you feel.

I get it!   I need a little help.   I don't get it.

Have a think about all the work you've done this term.
What went well?
What do you still need to practise?

I am confident with _____

_____

_____

_____

I will practise _____

_____

_____

_____

43

Block 1 Multiplication and division B

In this block, we explore **multiplication** and **division** and use our **times-table** knowledge.

Ten frames help when we're multiplying by 10

These ten frames show 16 × 10

Tens	Ones
10 10 10	1 1 1
10 10 10	1 1 1

We also use **place value charts** to multiply 2-digit numbers by 1-digit numbers.

This one represents 33 × 2

We use **part-whole models** to **partition** numbers when we are dividing. Here 78 has been partitioned into 60 and 18 to help work out the division 78 ÷ 6

60 ÷ 6 = 10   18 ÷ 6 = 3   10 + 3 = 13   78 ÷ 6 = 13

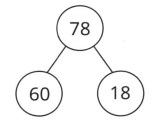

We use **number lines** to calculate divisions with remainders.

This one shows that 31 ÷ 4 = 7 r3

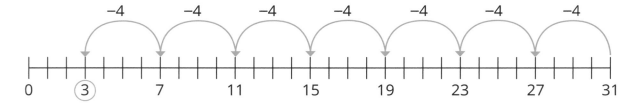

Here are some maths words that you'll see. Can you remember what they mean?

multiply   divide   times   sharing   grouping   equal parts

arrays   partition   remainder

Multiplication and division B Date:

Let's remember

1 $7 \times 8 = \boxed{}$

2 What is 48 divided by 4? $\boxed{}$

3 Use "odd" or "even" to complete the sentence.

All multiples of 2 are _____ numbers.

4 How many sides does a pentagon have? $\boxed{}$

Let's practise

1 Tiny is working out 18×10 using ten frames.

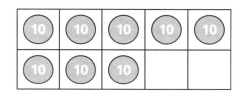

There are 18 counters, so $18 \times 10 = 18$

Do you agree with Tiny? _____

Explain your answer. _____

_____

2 Complete the multiplications.

a) $17 \times 10 = \boxed{}$

c) $23 \times 10 = \boxed{}$

b) $10 \times 19 = \boxed{}$

d) $36 \times 10 = \boxed{}$

3 Complete the related calculations.

a) $4 \times 5 = \boxed{}$

$40 \times 5 = \boxed{}$

b) $42 \div 6 = \boxed{}$

$420 \div 6 = \boxed{}$

4   Ron is working out 23 × 2 using a place value chart and counters.

Complete Ron's working.

Tens	Ones
10 10	1 1 1
10 10	1 1 1

$2 \times 3 = \boxed{}$

$2 \times 20 = \boxed{}$

$\boxed{} + \boxed{} = \boxed{}$

$23 \times 2 = \boxed{}$

5   Complete the multiplications.

a) $24 \times 3 = \boxed{}$ b) $3 \times 44 = \boxed{}$

6   Complete the number sentences to help you work out 53 × 4

Tens	Ones
10 10 10 10 10	1 1 1
10 10 10 10 10	1 1 1
10 10 10 10 10	1 1 1
10 10 10 10 10	1 1 1

$4 \times 3 = \boxed{}$

$4 \times 50 = \boxed{}$

$\boxed{} + \boxed{} = \boxed{}$

$53 \times 4 = \boxed{}$

7   Complete the multiplications.

a) $6 \times 15 = \boxed{}$ b) $26 \times 5 = \boxed{}$

8   A t-shirt costs £16 and a jumper costs £25

How much do 4 t-shirts and 5 jumpers cost altogether?   £ $\boxed{}$

🔍 Crack the code

Use your answers in the coloured boxes to crack the code.

132	360	5	212	70	130	190	200
p	l	m	l	i	y	u	t

Can you use the code word in a sentence?

____ ____ ____ ____ ____ ____ ____ ____

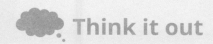 **Think it out**

The children at Brookside school are doing a quiz. The more answers they get correct, the more house points they win.

Score on quiz	Number of house points
0–3	5
4–7	12
8–12	20
13–18	35

How many house points were awarded in total?

Child	Score	House points given
Ron	17	
Mo	2	
Sam	15	
Eva	4	
Jack	16	
Teddy	9	
Tommy	1	
Jo	13	
Dora	10	
Annie	4	
Total		

How did you find these questions?   😞

Multiplication and division B

Date:

Let's remember

1 Use the fact 5 × 9 = 45 to work out 5 × 90 =

2 12 × 4 = 8 ×

3 32 ÷ 4 =

4 £1 + £3 + 20p + 50p = £ ☐ and ☐ p

Let's practise

1 Here are two arrays.

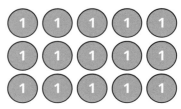   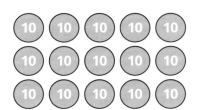

Think about the value of each counter.

a) What number does each array show?

b) Write a multiplication fact and a division fact for each array.

☐ × ☐ = ☐   ☐ × ☐ = ☐

☐ ÷ ☐ = ☐   ☐ ÷ ☐ = ☐

2 Use the facts 6 × 8 = 48 and 48 ÷ 8 = 6 to work out the calculations.

a) 60 × 8 =   c) 480 ÷ 8 =

b) 6 × 80 = ☐   d) 480 ÷ 6 =

3 Tiny is working out 560 ÷ 80

Do you agree with Tiny? _____

Explain your answer.

> I think the answer is 700. I know 56 ÷ 8 = 7. The numbers in the question are bigger so my answer will be bigger.

_____

_____

4 a) Use the part-whole model and complete the number sentences to help you to work out 56 ÷ 4

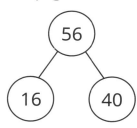

$16 ÷ 4 = \boxed{}$

$40 ÷ 4 = \boxed{}$

$\boxed{} + \boxed{} = \boxed{}$

$56 ÷ 4 = \boxed{}$

b) Use the method from part a) to work out 51 ÷ 3

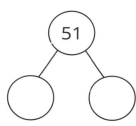

$\boxed{} ÷ \boxed{} = \boxed{}$

$\boxed{} ÷ \boxed{} = \boxed{}$

$\boxed{} + \boxed{} = \boxed{}$

$51 ÷ 3 = \boxed{}$

5 Work out the divisions.

a) $85 ÷ 5 = \boxed{}$

b) $76 ÷ 4 = \boxed{}$

6 What number between 90 and 100 can be divided equally by 2, 4 and 8? $\boxed{}$

🔍 Crack the code

Use your answers in the coloured boxes to crack the code.

15	19	480	10	17	6	80	8
v	n	i	i	o	d	s	i

> Explain what the code word means to someone.

_____ _____ _____ _____ _____ _____ _____ _____

 **Talk it out**

Eva is working out 92 ÷ 4

She starts by partitioning 92

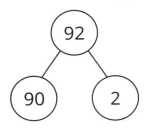 

Explain to someone in your home why partitioning 92 in this way is not helpful to work out this division.

Suggest a better way to partition 92

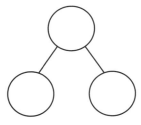

Is there only one way to partition 92 to make it easier to divide by 4?

 Partitioning 92 into 90 and 2 isn't helpful because . . .
I will partition 92 into . . . and . . .

 Think it out

 I think that all these numbers can be divided by 4 because they end in a 4

| 44 | 54 | 64 | 74 | 84 | 94 |

Can you tell if Mo is correct without working out the answers?

Try to divide all the numbers by 4 to convince Mo of your thinking.

How did you find these questions?

Multiplication and division B

Date:

Let's remember

1 $65 \div 5 =$ ☐

2 $28 \times 6 =$ ☐

3 $3 \times 4 + 5 \times 4 =$ ☐

4 10 more than 74 is ☐

Let's practise

1 Sam is using lolly sticks to work out $20 \div 3$

a) How many triangles has Sam made? ☐

b) How many lolly sticks are left over? ☐

A remainder is what is left over when we divide a number.

c) $20 \div 3 =$ ☐ remainder ☐

2 Use the number lines to help you to complete the divisions.

a) $19 \div 5 =$ ☐ remainder ☐

```
├─┼─┼─┼─┼─┼─┼─┼─┼─┼─┼─┼─┼─┼─┼─┼─┼─┼─┤
0  1  2  3  4  5  6  7  8  9  10 11 12 13 14 15 16 17 18 19
```

b) $19 \div 4 =$ ☐ remainder ☐

```
├─┼─┼─┼─┼─┼─┼─┼─┼─┼─┼─┼─┼─┼─┼─┼─┼─┼─┤
0  1  2  3  4  5  6  7  8  9  10 11 12 13 14 15 16 17 18 19
```

51

3   Work out the divisions.

a) 26 ÷ 4 = [ ] remainder [ ]   c) 44 ÷ 3 = [ ] remainder [ ]

b) 31 ÷ 5 = [ ] remainder [ ]   d) 54 ÷ 4 = [ ] remainder [ ]

4   Tiny has 2 dandelions.

Sam has 3 times as many dandelions.

How many dandelions do they have altogether? [ ]

Tiny [ ]

Sam [ ][ ][ ]

5   Mo has 5 hats and 3 scarves.

How many possible hat and scarf combinations can Mo make? [ ]

Crack the code

Use your answers in the coloured boxes to crack the code.

32	3	6	8	4	13
i	d	v	e	i	d

Can you use the code word in a sentence?

_____ _____ _____ _____ _____ _____

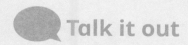 **Talk it out**

Use pencils to show someone in your family how to divide with remainders.

Show them the following divisions by making squares or triangles with your pencils.

| 10 ÷ 3 | | 15 ÷ 4 |

Draw your pencils.

 For the first division, I have made ... complete pencil triangles. There is ... pencil remaining. So 10 ÷ 3 is ... remainder ...

 Think it out

All numbers that end in a 0 or a 5 can be divided by 5 with no remainders.

Use Eva's fact to work out the remainders for these divisions without doing any calculations.

| 73 ÷ 5 | | 91 ÷ 5 | | 279 ÷ 5 |

Find a number between 300 and 400 that has a remainder of 2 when it is divided by 5

Find a number between 750 and 850 that has a remainder of 3 when it is divided by 5

Is it possible to have a remainder of 5 or 6 when you divide a number by 5? Explain why or why not.

_____

How did you find these questions?

Block 2 Length and perimeter

In this block, we explore measuring **length** and finding the **perimeters** of shapes. The perimeter is the distance around a shape.

We use rulers to take **measurements** in **centimetres** and **millimetres**.
This line is 3 cm and 7 mm long.

375 cm	
3 m	75 cm

We use **bar models** to help us find **equivalent** lengths. This one shows that 375 cm is equivalent to 3 m and 75 cm.

We use **addition** and **subtraction** to solve length problems. **Partitioning** and using **number bonds** to 10 and 100 will help us!

Height of the tower:
26 cm + 57 cm = 70 cm + 13 cm = 83 cm

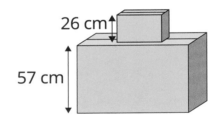

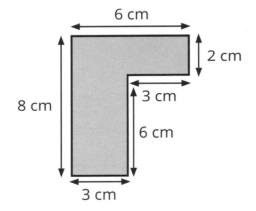

We will also work out the **perimeter** of a shape by adding the lengths of its sides. The perimeter of this shape is 28 cm.

Here are some maths words that you'll see. Can you remember what they mean?

measurements   metres (m)   centimetres (cm)   millimetres (mm)

equivalent   addition   subtraction   number bonds   perimeter

Length and perimeter

Let's remember

1 87 ÷ 8 = ☐ remainder ☐

2 84 ÷ 4 = ☐

3 Use "double" or "half" to complete the sentence.

The 8 times-table is _____ the 4 times-table.

4 10 less than 108 is ☐

Let's practise

1 What is the length of each line in centimetres?

a) 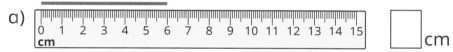 ☐ cm

b)  ☐ cm

2 Use a ruler to measure each line in millimetres.

a) 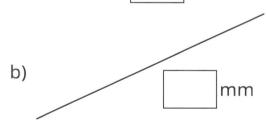 ☐ mm

b) ☐ mm

3 How tall is Tiny?

Tiny is ☐ cm and ☐ mm tall.

55

4   Teddy says the toy car is longer than the toy train.

a) Is Teddy correct? _____

b) Why do you think Teddy thought the car was longer than the train?

_____

_____

c) How long are the train and the car?   Train ☐ cm   Car ☐ cm

5   Put these lengths in order, starting with the shortest.

1 centimetre	1 metre	1 millimetre

_____

6   Kim is 143 cm tall.

Jack is 1 m and 49 cm tall.

Ron is 5 cm taller than Kim.

Ron's younger sister is 57 cm shorter than Jack.

a) How tall is Ron? ☐ cm

b) How tall is Ron's sister? ☐ cm

🔍 Crack the code

Use your answers in the coloured boxes to crack the code.

148	10	3	98	11	92	9
r	s	e	m	a	e	u

Can you explain what the code word means?

___ ___ ___ ___ ___ ___ ___

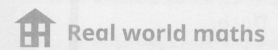 **Real world maths**

Estimate how tall some items are in your house. Then measure to check. Write your estimates and measurements in the table.

Item	Estimate	Actual
table	1 m	95 cm

I think the table is 1 m tall.

How close were your estimates?

Write each height in centimetres and in metres and centimetres.

_____

_____

_____

_____

_____

Can you write all the heights in order, starting with the shortest?

_____

_____

_____

Remember, 100 cm = 1 m.

How did you find these questions?   😞

Length and perimeter

Date:

Let's remember

1   Which is longer, 18 cm or 18 mm? _____

2   Annie has 4 t-shirts and 5 pairs of shorts.

How many different combinations of outfits can Annie make? ☐

3   32 × 7 = ☐

4   35p + ☐ p = £1

Let's practise

1   There are 10 mm in 1 cm and 100 cm in 1 m.

1 cm
10 mm

1 m
100 cm

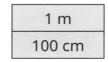

mm = millimetre, cm = centimetre, m = metre

Use the bar models to complete the sentences.

a)

1 cm	1 cm	1 cm	1 cm

☐ mm is equal to 4 cm

b)

10 mm	10 mm	10 mm	10 mm	10 mm	10 mm	10 mm

70 mm is equal to ☐ cm

c)

100 cm	100 cm	100 cm	100 cm	100 cm

500 cm is equal to ☐ m

2   Complete the sentences.

a) 10 mm = ☐ cm

b) 30 mm = ☐ cm

c) ☐ mm = 9 cm

d) 100 cm = ☐ m

e) 700 cm = ☐ m

f) ☐ cm = 6 m

3   Write "longer" or "shorter" to complete the sentences.

   a) 3 m is _____ than 299 cm.

   b) 95 mm is _____ than 10 cm.

   c) 1 m 70 cm is _____ than 107 cm.

4   Whitney buys 3 lengths of ribbon.

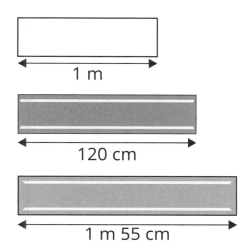

1 m

120 cm

1 m 55 cm

   a) What is the total length of the white, green and blue ribbons?

   [   ] cm

   b) Tommy buys a yellow ribbon that is 65 cm longer than Whitney's
       blue ribbon. What is the length of Tommy's ribbon?

   [   ] cm

Crack the code

Use your answers in the coloured boxes to crack the code.

375	20	3	220	5	600
t	l	n	h	e	g

Can you use
the code word in
a sentence?

____ ____ ____ ____ ____ ____

Think it out

$100 \text{ cm} = 1 \text{ m}$

Use this fact to write each length as a fraction of a metre.

$50 \text{ cm} = \dfrac{\boxed{}}{\boxed{}} \text{ m}$

$25 \text{ cm} = \dfrac{\boxed{}}{\boxed{}} \text{ m}$

Real world maths

A bus is about 2 and a half cars long.

A car is about 3 m long.

About how long is a bus in whole metres? _____

About how long is a bus in metres and centimetres? _____

About how long are 3 buses parked end to end? _____

How did you find these questions?

Length and perimeter

Date:

Let's remember

1 How many centimetres are there in 5 metres? ☐ cm

2 Which is shorter, 8 mm or 8 cm? _____

3 68 divided by 4 = ☐

4 Complete the number track.

	6	9				21

Let's practise

1 Tiny and Jo are working out the perimeter of this rectangle.

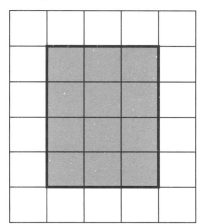

 The perimeter is 12 cm. I counted the coloured squares inside the rectangle.

 The perimeter is 14 cm. I counted the squares around the sides of the rectangle.

Who do you agree with? _____

Why? _____

2 Work out the perimeter of these rectangles.

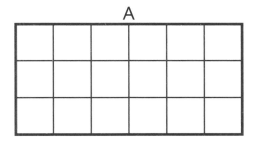

A

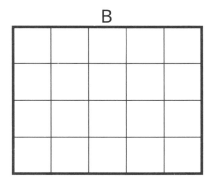

B

C

A = ☐ cm

B = ☐ cm

C = ☐ cm

3   Work out the perimeter of each shape.

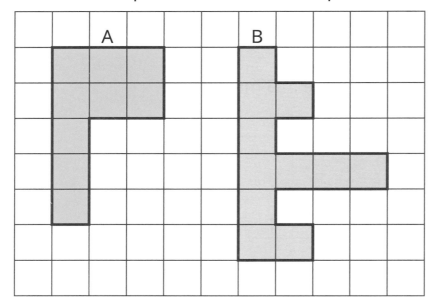

A = ☐ cm

B = ☐ cm

4   Use a ruler to measure the perimeter of this shape.

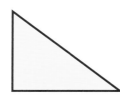

Perimeter = ☐ cm

Measure to the nearest centimetre.

5   Work out the perimeter of each shape.

a)
12 cm   12 cm
12 cm   12 cm
12 cm

☐ cm

b)
25 cm
20 cm
30 cm   50 cm

☐ cm

6   A rectangle has a perimeter of 48 cm.

The length of the rectangle is 14 cm.

What is the width of the rectangle? ☐ cm

🔍 **Crack the code**

Use your answers in the coloured boxes to crack the code.

10	16	17	60	24
h	i	w	t	d

Can you use the code word in a sentence?

____ ____ ____ ____ ____

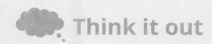 **Think it out**

On the grid, draw as many different shapes as you can with a perimeter of 18 cm.

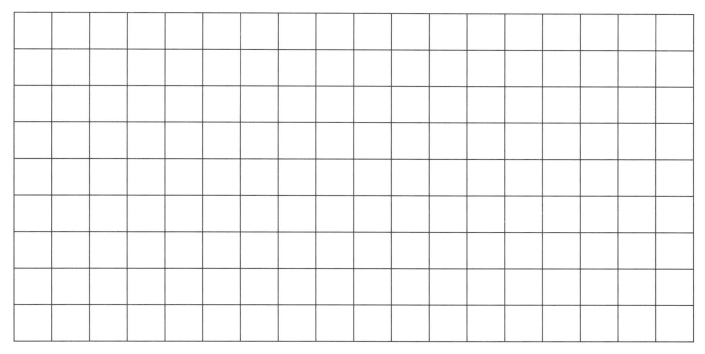

 Real world maths

Think about the rooms in your home or school.

Estimate the perimeters for two of the rooms. Record your guesses below.

I estimate the perimeter of Room 1 is _____

I estimate the perimeter of Room 2 is _____

Now use a tape measure or metre stick to measure the perimeters of the rooms.

> You will probably need someone to help you.

The actual perimeter of Room 1 is _____

The actual perimeter of Room 2 is _____

How close were your estimates?

How did you find these questions?

In this block, we explore finding **fractions** – that's when we find **part** of something, or a number of parts of something.

We use **bar models** to represent the fractions.
Here's one! It has been divided into 5 **equal parts**, or fifths.

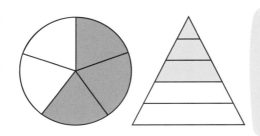

We identify when **fractions of shapes** have been shaded correctly. Fractions are equal parts, so $\frac{3}{5}$ of the circle has been shaded, but the triangle has not been divided into equal fifths.

We use **part-whole models** to help us find the two parts of the whole.
The missing fraction here is $\frac{3}{7}$

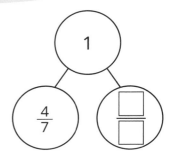

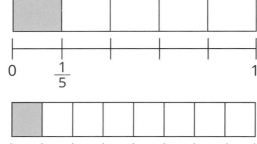

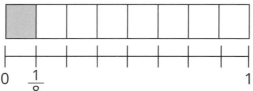

$0 \quad \frac{1}{5} \qquad\qquad\qquad 1$

$0 \quad \frac{1}{8} \qquad\qquad\qquad 1$

Number lines are useful to help us **order** and **compare** fractions. These ones clearly show that $\frac{1}{5}$ is greater than $\frac{1}{8}$

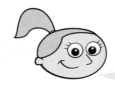

Here are some maths words that you'll see.
Can you remember what they mean?

part   whole   denominator   numerator   greater than

less than   equal parts   compare   order   equivalent

Fractions A

Date:

Let's remember

1 The length of a rectangle is 12 cm.
   The width of the rectangle is 7 cm.
   What is the perimeter of the rectangle? ☐ cm

2 How many centimetres are equal to 60 mm? ☐ cm

3 Jo has 3 pencils.
   Max has 5 times as many pencils as Jo.
   How many pencils do they have altogether? ☐

4 Write 43 in words. _____

Let's practise

1 Complete the sentences for each bar model.

   a)

   The whole is split into ☐ equal parts.

   The fraction shaded is $\frac{☐}{☐}$

   The numerator is ☐

   The denominator is ☐

   b)

   The whole is split into ☐ equal parts.

   The fraction shaded is $\frac{☐}{☐}$

   The numerator is ☐

   The denominator is ☐

2   a) What fraction of each bar model is shaded?

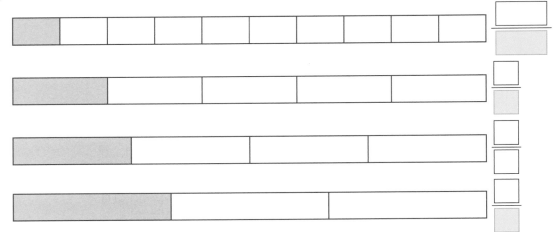

b) Write > or < to compare the fractions.

$\frac{1}{4}$ ◯ $\frac{1}{10}$ $\frac{1}{3}$ ◯ $\frac{1}{5}$ $\frac{1}{5}$ ◯ $\frac{1}{4}$

3   Draw a diagram to show that $\frac{1}{2}$ is greater than $\frac{1}{3}$

4   Write the fractions in ascending order.

$\frac{1}{8}$	$\frac{1}{3}$	$\frac{1}{5}$	$\frac{1}{10}$

_____

5   Circle the greater fraction.

$\frac{3}{82}$ $\frac{3}{64}$

Explain how you know.

_____

Crack the code

Use your answers in the coloured boxes to crack the code.

5	3	9	38	10	18	6	2
o	n	c	f	i	r	t	a

Can you explain what the code word means?

_____ _____ _____ _____ _____ _____ _____ _____

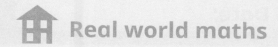

Real world maths

Fractions appear in lots of different places.

This week, try to spot as many fractions as you can.

Record what you find in the space below.

Think about food labels, road signs and recipes to get you started.

Are the fractions always written in the same way?

Talk it out

Teach someone in your home all about fractions.

Answer these questions for them.

- What is the numerator?

- What is the denominator?

- How do you compare two fractions?
  For example, $\frac{1}{3}$ and $\frac{1}{7}$ or $\frac{3}{5}$ and $\frac{2}{5}$

- When you are drawing a bar model of a fraction, why do you need to split the bar into equal parts?

How did you find these questions?   😞

Fractions A

Date:

Let's remember

1   Which is smaller, $\frac{1}{4}$ or $\frac{1}{5}$? $\frac{\Box}{\Box}$

2   A square has a side length of 12 mm.
    What is the perimeter of the square? ☐ mm

3   Which is longer, 1 m 28 cm or 3 m 28 cm? ☐ m ☐ cm

4   How many faces does a cube have? ☐

Let's practise

1   Complete the sentence for each shape.

   a)

   The whole is split into ☐ equal parts.

   ☐ parts are shaded.

   The fraction shaded is $\frac{\Box}{\Box}$

   b)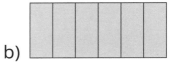

   The whole is split into ☐ equal parts.

   ☐ parts are shaded.

   The fraction shaded is $\frac{\Box}{\Box}$

2   Complete the sentences for the bar model.

   ☐ fifths + ☐ fifths = ☐ fifths

   ☐ fifths is the same as 1 whole.

3 Complete the part-whole models.

a)

b)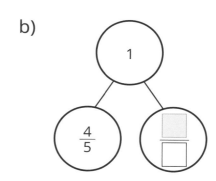

4 Compare the fractions using < or >. Use the bar models to help you.

a) $\frac{3}{4}$ ◯ $\frac{1}{4}$

b) $\frac{5}{7}$ ◯ $\frac{3}{7}$

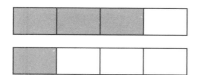

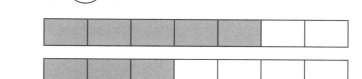

5 Write <, > or = to compare the fractions.

a) $\frac{8}{21}$ ◯ $\frac{18}{21}$

b) $\frac{4}{4}$ ◯ $\frac{10}{10}$

c) $\frac{3}{4}$ ◯ $\frac{3}{5}$

6 Order each set of fractions, starting with the greatest.

a) $\frac{7}{8}$ $\frac{1}{8}$ $\frac{8}{8}$ $\frac{3}{8}$

b) $\frac{5}{6}$ $\frac{5}{9}$ $\frac{5}{7}$ $\frac{5}{11}$

7 Draw a diagram to show that $\frac{5}{6}$ is greater than $\frac{5}{8}$

Crack the code

Use your answers in the coloured boxes to crack the code.

10	1	11	3	7	48	6	5	2
a	t	r	e	o	n	m	r	u

Can you use the code word in a sentence?

___ ___ ___   ___ ___ ___ ___ ___

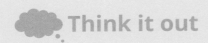 Think it out

Roll a dice to get two different numbers.

Use the smaller number as the numerator and the greater number as the denominator, e.g. $\frac{3}{5}$

- Write a fraction that is smaller than your fraction.

- Write a fraction that is greater than your fraction.

- Repeat at least 5 times and record your answers.

 Talk it out

Use the word bank to explain to someone in your home how to:

- compare fractions with the same numerator,

- compare fractions with the same denominator.

numerator	denominator	greater	smaller

... is greater than ... because ...
... is smaller than ... because...
When the denominators are the same, I compare by ...

How did you find these questions?

Fractions

Date:

Let's remember

1. How many eighths are there in 1 whole? ☐

2. Tommy cuts a piece of ribbon into 4 equal parts.

   What fraction of the piece of ribbon is each part? $\frac{\square}{\square}$

3. Which is shorter, 1 m 28 cm or 3 m 12 cm? ☐ m ☐ cm

4. 365 + 20 = ☐

Let's practise

1. Complete each number line.

   a)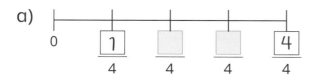

   What fraction comes next? How do you know?

   b)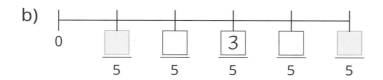

   c)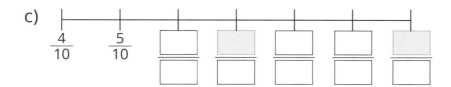

   d)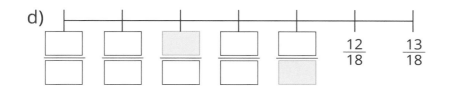

   "Equivalent" means equal in value.

2. Sam thinks $\frac{2}{6}$ is equivalent to $\frac{4}{8}$ because when you add 2 to both the numerator and the denominator you get $\frac{4}{8}$

   Do you agree with Sam? _____

   Explain your answer. _____

3 Use the number lines to help you complete the sentences.

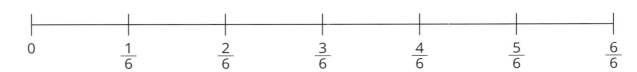

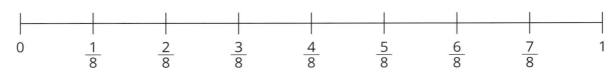

a) $\frac{1}{6}$ is less than $\frac{\square}{\square}$

b) $\frac{5}{8}$ is _____ than $\frac{1}{2}$

c) $\frac{1}{2}$ is equivalent to $\frac{\square}{\square}$

4 Write the equivalent fractions shown by each bar model.

a)

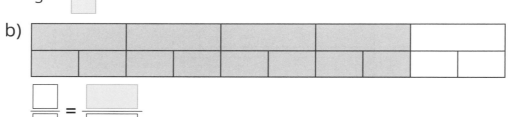

$\frac{2}{3} = \frac{\square}{\square}$

b)

$\frac{\square}{\square} = \frac{\square}{\square}$

Q Crack the code

Use your answers in the coloured boxes to crack the code.

10	18	2	6	7	385	8	9	5	3	1
n	t	e	o	i	d	r	a	m	n	o

Can you use the code word in a sentence?

____ ____ ____ ____ ____ ____ ____ ____ ____ ____ ____

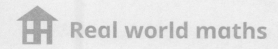 **Real world maths**

Cut six strips of paper, all the same length.

Fold each of the strips into different numbers of equal parts.

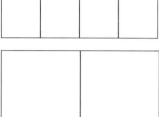

A good length for your strips would be about 15 cm.

The top strip is folded into quarters and the lower one is folded in half. So I can see $\frac{1}{2}$ is equivalent to $\frac{2}{4}$

How many different equivalent fractions can you find?

_____

 Think it out

Create your own number line for eighths, starting at zero and ending at $\frac{8}{8}$

Then estimate where on the number line these fractions would go.

$\frac{9}{10}$ $\frac{1}{3}$ $\frac{5}{9}$

Explain your decisions.

_____

How did you find these questions?

In this block, we explore **mass** and **capacity**. We practise using **number lines** to help us read **scales** correctly.

The arrow is pointing to 75 on this number line.

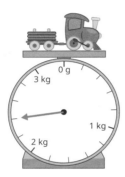

We read scales to find the **mass** of objects. Remember that the mass is the amount of matter an object contains. We measure this using **grams** and **kilograms**.

This toy train has a mass of 2 kg and 400 g.

Balance scales help us to **compare** different masses.

The sphere is **heavier** than the cube. The cube is **lighter** than the sphere.

We measure **volume** and **capacity** using **litres** and **millilitres**.

The total capacity of this jug is 3 litres, but the volume of water it contains is 2 litres and 400 millilitres.

Here are some maths words that you'll see. Can you remember what they mean?

capacity   volume   mass   weight   scale   grams

kilograms   litres   millilitres   heavier/lighter   full/empty

Mass and capacity

Date:

Let's remember

1   $\frac{1}{2} = \frac{\square}{8}$

2   Which is greater, $\frac{5}{12}$ or $\frac{7}{12}$?

3   The perimeter of a square is 40 cm.

What is the side length of the square? [ ] cm

4   How many vertices does a cube have? [ ]

Let's practise

1   Label the intervals on each number line.

a)

0   100

b)

0   100

2   What is the mass of each object?

a)   b)

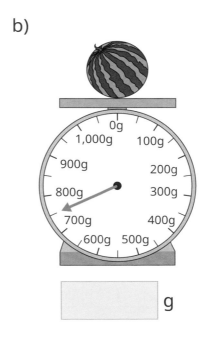

[ ] g   [ ] g

3 Jack thinks the mass of the bag is 2 kg 500 g.

Mo thinks the mass of the bag is 2 kg 400 g.

Who do you agree with? _____

Explain your answer. _____

_____

4 Complete the number sentences.

a) [   ] g = 1 kg

b) 300 g + [   ] g = 1 kg

c) 450 g + [   ] g = 1 kg

d) [   ] g + 50 g = 1 kg

5 Complete the fractions.

a) 500 g = $\frac{\square}{\square}$ kg

b) 100 g = $\frac{\square}{\square}$ kg

c) 250 g = $\frac{\square}{\square}$ kg

6 Tiny finds the mass of a football on two different scales.

 The football is heavier on the second scale!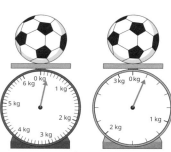

Do you agree with Tiny? _____

Explain your answer. _____

_____

🔍 Crack the code

Use your answers in the coloured boxes to crack the code.

2	8	1,000	10	400	950	750	7
a	i	g	m	l	r	o	k

Can you use the code word in a sentence?

____ ____ ____ ____ ____ ____ ____ ____

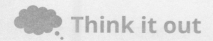 **Think it out**

Here are some weights.

Using the weights, how many different ways can you make 500 g?

Using the weights, how many different ways can you make 1 kg?

Talk it out

Here is a number line and a circular scale.

What is the same? What is different?

0   1,000

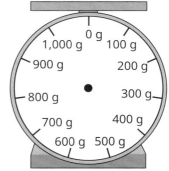

 The number line and the scale are the same because ...
They are different because ...

How did you find these questions?

Mass and capacity

Date:

Let's remember

1 How many grams are there in 1 kg? ⬚ g

2 What comes next?

$\frac{2}{5}, \frac{3}{5}, \frac{4}{5}$ $\frac{\square}{\square}$

3 Ron draws a bar model split into 10 equal parts. He shades 3 of the parts. What fraction of the bar model has he shaded? $\frac{\square}{\square}$

4 $25 \div \square = 5$

Let's practise

1 Write "heavier" or "lighter" to compare the objects.

The pineapple is _____ than the toy car.

The toy car is _____ than the pineapple.

2

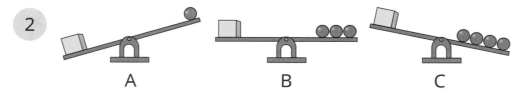

A   B   C

a) Tick the scale that shows items with an equal mass.

b) Complete the sentence.

1 cube has the same mass as ⬚ spheres.

3 Write < or > to compare the masses.

a) 300 g ◯ 700 g   c) 1 kg ◯ 999 g

b) 650 g ◯ 398 g   d) 10 g ◯ 10 kg

4 How much water is in each jug?

a) 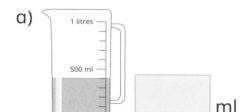 ◻ ml

b) 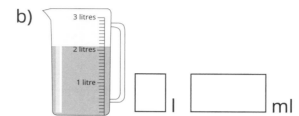 ◻ l ◻ ml

5 Each day, Sam's dog eats 150 g of biscuits in the morning and 250 g of biscuits in the evening.

a) How many grams of biscuits does Sam's dog eat in 1 day?

◻ g

b) How many grams of biscuits does Sam's dog eat in 2 days?

◻ g

6 Tiny is having a snack of dandelions. The mass of the bowl is 50 g.

The mass of the dandelions is 300 g.

Do you agree with Tiny? _____

Explain your answer. _____

🔍 Crack the code

Use your answers in the coloured boxes to crack the code.

800	5	3	400
s	m	a	s

Can you use the code word in a sentence?

_____ _____ _____ _____

Real world maths

Find a recipe for one of your favourite dishes.

Look at the masses of the ingredients.

Which has the greatest mass?

Cookbooks, food magazines or online are good places to look.

_____

Which has the smallest mass?

_____

Can you work out the total mass of all your dry ingredients?

_____

Ask an adult to help you read the recipe, if you need help.

You could even try weighing out and making your recipe with an adult.

Have fun!

 Think it out

The capacity of a water barrel is 9 l 500 ml.

Jo can use these containers to fill the barrel completely with water.

| 5 l | 3 l | 1 l | 250 ml |

Which containers could Jo use?

Is there more than one way of filling the barrel?

Which way would be the quickest?

How did you find these questions?

Mass and capacity

Date:

Let's remember

1 3 kg 450 g + 2 kg 128 g = ☐ kg ☐ g

2 The mass of a box is 1,000 g.

What is the mass of the box in kilograms? ☐ kg

3 Jack shades $\frac{3}{5}$ of a bar model. How much more does he need to shade

for the whole bar to be shaded? $\frac{☐}{☐}$

4 What is 9 cm – 5 cm? ☐ cm

Let's practise

1 Write the missing measurement on the scale on each jug.

a)
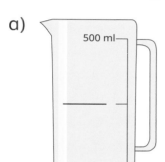
500 ml

b)

1,000 ml

c)
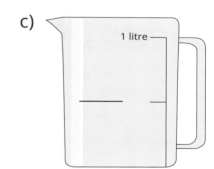
1 litre

2 Sam has 1 litre of juice.

1 litre

A cup can hold 200 millilitres of juice.

How many cups can Sam fill with her litre of juice? ☐

3 Complete the number sentences.

a) [   ] ml + 500 ml = 1 l

b) 750 ml + [   ] ml = 1 l

c) [   ] ml + 999 ml = 1 l

d) 100 ml + [   ] ml = 1 l

e) 520 ml + [   ] ml = 1 l

f) 1 l = 7 ml + [   ] ml

4 Complete the bar models.

a)
1 litre		
50 ml	400 ml	[ ] ml

b)
1 litre		
170 ml	[ ] ml	320 ml

5 Write <, > or = to compare the capacities.

a) 500 ml ◯ 490 ml

b) 1 l ◯ 1 ml

c) 2 l 300 ml ◯ 3 l 200 ml

d) $\frac{1}{2}$ l ◯ 500 ml

6 The capacities of 4 containers are shown.

5 l   2 l 300 ml   600 ml   200 ml

What is the total capacity of the 4 containers? [   ] l [   ] ml

---

Q Crack the code

Use your answers in the coloured boxes to crack the code.

5	900	4	100	578	993	2	500
a	i	p	y	c	t	a	c

Can you explain what the code word means?

_____ _____ _____ ___ _____ _____ _____ _____

Real world maths

A tablespoon can hold 15 ml of water.

Find a small container.

How many tablespoons of water will it take to fill it? _____

Keep a tally of the number of tablespoons of water you use to find the capacity of your container.

Talk it out

You have been learning about equivalent lengths, masses, volumes and capacities.

Write down as many facts as you can remember on cards.

10 mm = 1 cm

Ask someone to test you on them.

"Equivalent" means of equal value.

There are … millilitres in a litre.
There are … centimetres in a metre.
There are … grams in a kilogram.

How did you find these questions?

Time to reflect

Look back through the work you have done this term. Think about what you enjoyed and what you found easy or hard. Talk about this to your teacher or someone at home.

Look back at the multiplication questions on page 46. Use the table below to calculate 23 × 2

Tens	Ones
10 10	1 1 1
10 10	1 1 1

23 × 2 = ☐

How did you find this question? Circle one of the statements to show how you feel.

| I am confident and could teach someone else. | I think I understand but I need more practice. | I don't understand and need help. |

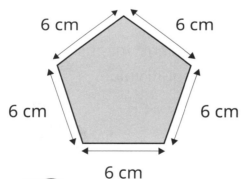

6 cm   6 cm

6 cm   6 cm

6 cm

Look back at finding the perimeter of shapes in Block 2. What is the perimeter of this shape?

Perimeter = ☐ cm

How did you find this? Colour in one of the faces to show how it made you feel.

I get it!

I need a little help.

I don't get it.

How did you find placing fractions on a number line on page 71?
Place $\frac{4}{9}$ and $\frac{6}{9}$ on the number line below.

0    $\frac{2}{9}$ $\frac{3}{9}$ $\frac{7}{9}$ $\frac{9}{9}$

 Circle one of the cards to show how it made you feel.

1	2	3	4
I found this hard and need some help.	I need some more practice.	I can do this well and didn't make any mistakes.	I am confident and could teach someone else.

Have a think about all the work you've done this term.
What went well?
What do you still need to practise?

I am confident with _____

_____

_____

_____

I will practise _____

_____

_____

_____

In this block, we explore **fractions** further. This time, we use **bar models** to help us **add** fractions.
This bar model represents $\frac{1}{7} + \frac{4}{7} = \frac{5}{7}$

We also use bar models to help us **subtract** fractions.

This is how I've represented $\frac{8}{9} - \frac{3}{9}$

We use **counters** to help us find **fractions of quantities**.
To find $\frac{1}{4}$ of 12, I have placed the counters onto a bar model that has four **equal parts**. $\frac{1}{4}$ of 12 is 3

Here are some maths words that you'll see.
Can you remember what they mean?

equal parts   numerator   denominator   fractions of quantities

addition   subtraction

Fractions B

Date:

Let's remember

1 400 ml + 200 ml = ⬚ ml

2 1 kg – 300 g = ⬚ g

3 $\frac{1}{5}$, $\frac{2}{5}$, $\frac{\square}{\square}$, $\frac{\square}{\square}$, $\frac{\square}{\square}$

4 How many sides does a hexagon have? ⬚

Let's practise

1 Use the bar model to help you work out $\frac{1}{9} + \frac{4}{9}$

$\frac{1}{9} + \frac{4}{9} = \frac{\square}{\square}$

2 Shade the bar model to work out the addition.

$\frac{4}{11} + \frac{3}{11} = \frac{\square}{\square}$

3 Complete the additions.

a) $\frac{1}{6} + \frac{4}{6} = \frac{\square}{\square}$

c) $\frac{3}{10} + \frac{4}{10} = \frac{\square}{\square}$

b) $\frac{\square}{\square} + \frac{3}{7} = \frac{6}{7}$

d) $\frac{1}{4} + \frac{3}{4} = \frac{\square}{\square} = \square$

> Can you write the answer to part d) in two different ways?

4 Use the bar model to help you work out $\frac{8}{11} - \frac{3}{11}$

$\frac{8}{11} - \frac{3}{11} = \frac{\square}{\square}$

5 Complete the subtractions.

a) $\dfrac{11}{12} - \dfrac{5}{12} = \dfrac{\boxed{}}{\boxed{}}$

c) $\dfrac{6}{7} - \dfrac{6}{7} = \dfrac{\boxed{}}{\boxed{}}$

b) $\dfrac{4}{5} - \dfrac{3}{5} = \dfrac{\boxed{}}{\boxed{}}$

d) $1 - \dfrac{3}{8} = \dfrac{\boxed{}}{\boxed{}}$

6 Complete each part-whole model.

a)
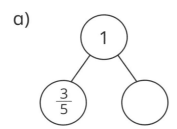

b)
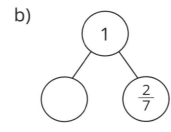

c)
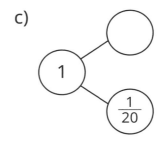

7 Tiny is working out $\dfrac{367}{450} - \dfrac{366}{450}$

It will take me a long time because the numbers are so big!

Explain to Tiny why this question can be answered quickly.

_____

_____

_____

🔍 Crack the code

Use your answers in the coloured boxes to crack the code.

Can you use the code word in a sentence?

4	6	3	8	5	700	11	7
n	h	e	s	v	s	t	e

_____ _____ _____ _____ _____ _____ _____ _____

 **Think it out**

Choose fractions to complete the calculation.

$$\frac{\square}{\square} + \frac{\square}{\square} + \frac{\square}{\square} = \frac{27}{30}$$

Is there more than one answer?

How many different ways can you find?

 Real world maths

Check how many pages your reading book has.

Write the fraction of the total pages
you have read so far.

I have read $\dfrac{\square}{\square}$ of my book.

Work out the fraction that you have left to read.

I have $\dfrac{\square}{\square}$ of my book left to read.

My reading book has 201 pages.

I have read 10 pages so I have
read $\frac{10}{201}$ of my book.

I have $\frac{191}{201}$ of my book left to read.

How did you find these questions?

Fractions B

Date:

Let's remember

1 $\frac{2}{3} + \frac{\square}{\square} = 1$

2 $\frac{4}{13} + \frac{5}{13} = \frac{\square}{\square}$

3 $\boxed{}$ g = 1 kg

4 76 has $\boxed{}$ tens and $\boxed{}$ ones

Let's practise

1 Complete the number sentence.

   $\frac{1}{2}$ of 6 = $\boxed{}$

2 Draw counters in each bar model to help you complete the number sentences.

   a) $\frac{1}{2}$ of 10 = $\boxed{}$

   b) $\frac{1}{4}$ of 12 = $\boxed{}$

   c) $\frac{1}{4}$ of 4 = $\boxed{}$

   d) $\frac{1}{5}$ of 10 = $\boxed{}$

3 Complete the number sentences.

   a) $\frac{1}{4}$ of 20 = $\boxed{}$ c) $\frac{1}{4}$ of 44 = $\boxed{}$

   b) $\frac{1}{5}$ of 100 = $\boxed{}$ d) $\frac{1}{3}$ of 60 = $\boxed{}$

4   Max is drawing counters to work out $\frac{2}{3}$ of 39

a) Complete Max's drawing.   b) What is $\frac{2}{3}$ of 39?

5   Complete the number sentences.

a) $\frac{3}{4}$ of 40 = ☐   c) $\frac{2}{3}$ of 27 = ☐

b) $\frac{2}{5}$ of 35 = ☐   d) $\frac{4}{5}$ of 100 = ☐

6   Dora has £45

She spends $\frac{2}{5}$ of her money on a t-shirt.

How much money does Dora have left?   £ ☐

7   Jack has some counters.

Here are $\frac{3}{4}$ of Jack's counters.

How many counters does Jack have in total? ☐

🔍 Crack the code

Use your answers in the coloured boxes to crack the code.

26	5	80	12	3	6	30	1	20
t	e	o	n	o	p	i	r	a

Can you explain what the code word means?

_____ _____ _____ _____ _____ _____ _____ _____ _____

 **Talk it out**

Teddy is using 12 pieces of pasta to explain how to find a fraction of an amount. What could he say?

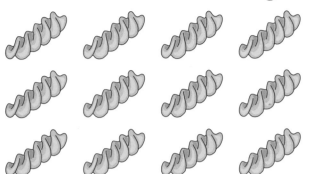

I'm going to use words such as "numerator", "denominator" and "equal parts" in my explanation.

 To find a fraction of an amount I ...

The numerator is the top part of a fraction. The denominator is the bottom part.

Use some small objects from around your home to explain how to find a fraction of an amount.

 **Think it out**

What do the star and heart represent?

$\frac{1}{4}$ of ⭐ = 30

$\frac{3}{5}$ of ❤ = 240

⭐ + ❤ = ☐

Can you create your own fraction puzzle like this one?

How did you find these questions?   😞

92

In this block, we explore **money**.
We find different amounts of
pounds and **pence**.
I've found £1 and 30p.

We count **coins** and **notes** to find **total amounts** of money.
I've counted £10 and 75p!

£5 and 30p

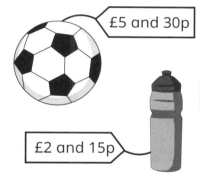

£2 and 15p

We use **addition** to find the total amount spent.
I can calculate the total by adding the pounds
first and then the pence.
£5 and 30p + £2 and 15p = £7 and 45p

We use **subtraction** and **number lines** to calculate
change. If I use a £10 note to buy the items, I will get
£2 and 55p change.

£10 – £7 and 45p = £2 and 55p

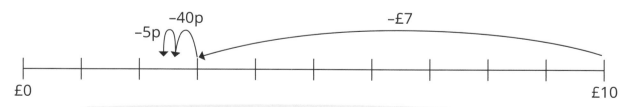

Here are some maths words that you'll see.
Can you remember what they mean?

coins   notes   amount   spent   total   change   pounds   pence

Money

Date:

Let's remember

1 $\frac{1}{5}$ of an amount is 10. What is the whole amount?

2 Seven tenths subtract four tenths is $\frac{\boxed{}}{\boxed{}}$

3 $\frac{1}{2} = \frac{\boxed{}}{4}$

4 Write the odd numbers that are less than 5 _____

Let's practise

1 Circle the amounts.

a) 15p

b) £1 and 50p

c) 64p

How many ways can you find to make 64p?

2 Ron has this money.

How much money does Ron have? £ $\boxed{}$

3   Count the money.

a)

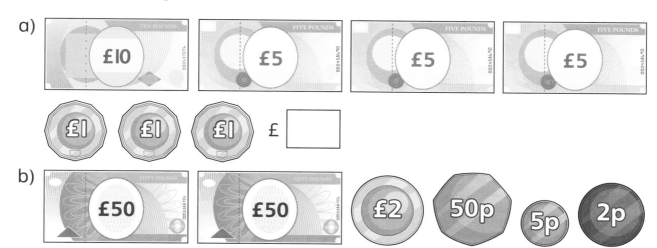

£ ☐

b)

£ ☐ and ☐ p

4   Complete the sentence.

There are ☐ pence in £1

5   How many of each type of coin do you need to make £1?

a) ☐ 20p coins   b) ☐ 10p coins   c) ☐ 5p coins

6   Write each amount in pounds and pence.

a) 136p = £ ☐ and ☐ p   c) 799p = £ ☐ and ☐ p

b) 450p = £ ☐ and ☐ p   d) 106p = £ ☐ and ☐ p

7   Mo and Jack both have £1 and 25p.

Mo has 3 coins.

Jack has 7 coins.

a) Which coins does Mo have? _____

b) Which coins could Jack have? _____

Crack the code

Use your answers in the coloured boxes to crack the code.

6	57	2	5	50	4
e	a	h	n	c	g

Can you use the code word in a sentence?

_____ _____ _____ _____ _____ _____

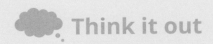 **Think it out**

Eva has this money.

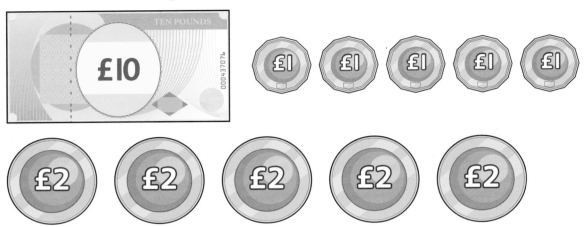

Sam has the same amount of money, but he has two notes and some coins.

Which coins and notes could Sam have?

Find more than one possibility.

How did you find these questions?   😞

Money

Date:

Let's remember

1   £□ = 100p

2   $1 - \frac{3}{8} = \frac{\square}{\square}$

3   800 g + 300 g = □ kg and □ g

4   5 × 36 = □

Let's practise

1   Ron buys a bag of apples and a bag of pears.

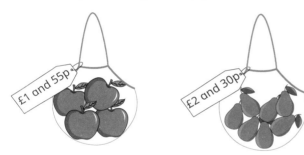

£1 and 55p

£2 and 30p

Complete the sentences to work out how much Ron spends.

£□ + £□ = £□

□ p + □ p = □ p

Ron spends £□ and □ p

First, I can add the pounds and then the pence.

2   Find the total amounts of money.

a) £3 and 31p + £3 and 52p = £□ and □ p

b) £2 and 7p + £5 and 46p = £□ and □ p

c) £4 and 80p + £8 and 15p = £□ and □ p

d) £10 and 36p + £11 and 49p = £□ and □ p

3   Complete the bar models.

a)

£1 and 90p	
£1	☐ p

b)

£5 and 24p		
£3 and 13p	£ ☐ and	☐ p

4   Alex buys these items.

£2   £5 and 10p

A number line can help you to work out how much change I will get.

How much change will Alex get from a £10 note? _____

5   Mo uses a £5 note to buy two of these items.

He gets £3 and 45p change.

£85p   £1 and 50p   £1 and 95p   70p

Which two items does Mo buy?

_____

🔍 **Crack the code**

Can you use the code words in a sentence?

Use your answers in the coloured boxes to crack the code.

90	3	5	180	11	85
d	u	p	o	s	n

_____ _____ _____ _____ _____ _____

 **Real world maths**

A family order lunch from this menu.

They order 2 cheese sandwiches, 1 egg sandwich and 1 baked potato.

They pay with a £20 note.

Draw the notes and coins that the family get as change.

Is there more than one way of showing this?

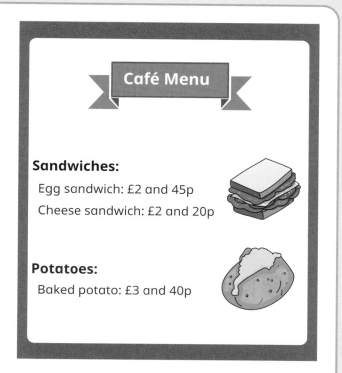

Café Menu

Sandwiches:
Egg sandwich: £2 and 45p
Cheese sandwich: £2 and 20p

Potatoes:
Baked potato: £3 and 40p

 Talk it out

Whitney buys 2 train tickets.

One ticket costs £6 and 35p and the other one costs £12 and 75p.

She pays with one £10 note, one £5 note and three £2 coins.

Work out how much change she gets.

Explain to someone how to solve this problem.

 First, I … next I …, then I …

How did you find these questions?

In this block, we explore telling the **time**. We use the words **"to"** and **"past"** to say the times shown on different **clocks**. The first clock shows the time 10 minutes to 4. The second clock shows the time 5 minutes past 9.

We also use **digital clocks** to tell the time and use **am** and **pm** to describe in which part of the day something happened. I had breakfast at 7:00 am and I went to bed at 7:45 pm.

JUNE

M	T	W	Th	F	Sa	Su
1	2	3	4	5	6	7
8	9	10	11	12	13	14
15	16	17	18	19	20	21
22	23	24	25	26	27	28
29	30					

We use **calendars** to identify the **days**, **weeks** and **months** in a **year**. This year my birthday is on a Saturday!

Number lines help us work out how long something took. Here's one that shows a journey took 43 minutes.

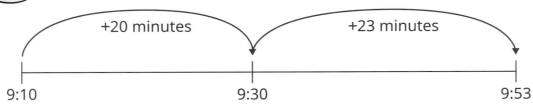

+20 minutes   +23 minutes

9:10   9:30   9:53

Here are some maths words that you'll see. Can you remember what they mean?

minutes   hours   days   weeks   months   years
to   past   am   pm   clock   calendar

Time

Date:

Let's remember

1 £3 and 35p – £1 and 14p = £ ⬚ and ⬚ p

2 What is $\frac{2}{3}$ of 24 cm? ⬚ cm

3 $\frac{1}{2} = \frac{\square}{6}$

4 Complete the number track.

3	6	9			

Let's practise

1 Write the Roman numerals as numbers.

a) III ⬚   c) X ⬚   e) VII ⬚

b) V ⬚   d) IX ⬚   f) IV ⬚

2 What time is shown on each clock?

a) ⬚ minutes past ⬚

b) ⬚ minutes past ⬚

c) ⬚ minutes past ⬚

3 This clock shows 40 minutes past 4. Complete the sentence to say the time in another way.

 ☐ minutes to ☐

4 What time is shown on each clock?

a)

☐ minutes past ☐

b)

☐ minutes past ☐

5 Draw hands on the clocks to show the times.

a) 28 minutes past 3

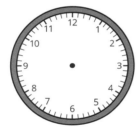

b) 14 minutes past 11

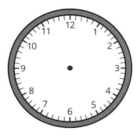

6 The hour hand is midway between an odd number and a multiple of 3.

What time could it be? Explain your thinking.

_____

There is more than one possible answer.

🔍 **Crack the code**

Use your answers in the coloured boxes to crack the code.

9	2	3	20	16	7	10
t	s	i	u	m	n	e

Can you use the code word in a sentence?

_____ _____ _____ _____ _____ _____ _____

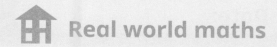 **Real world maths**

Create your own clock!

1. Get a paper plate or trace a circle on a sheet of paper and cut it out.

2. Write the clock numbers in the correct positions.

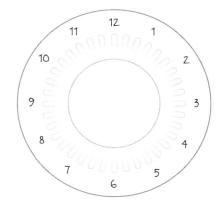

3. Cut out two hands (one long and one short.)
   If you have some sticky tack, you could stick
   the hands in the middle of the clock.

Have fun practising different times.

Why not:

• move the hands and tell someone what time it is,

• ask what time it is and see if you can show it on your clock,

• read the digital time and show it on your clock,

• think about some times that are important to you and show them on
  your clock.

How did you find these questions?   😟

Time

Date:

Let's remember

1   What is another way to say forty minutes past seven?

_____

2   £2 and 38p + £3 and 42p = £ ☐ and ☐ p

3   $\frac{4}{13} + \frac{6}{13} = \frac{\boxed{}}{\boxed{}}$

4   How long is the line?   _____

Give your answer to the nearest whole centimetre. ☐ cm

Let's practise

1   Write "am" or "pm" to complete Mo's bedtime.

7:15 _____

2   Tick the later time.

| 8:55 am | 8:55 pm |

3   Tick the earlier time.

| 11:00 am | 6:30 pm |

4   Complete the sentences.

a) There are ☐ days in 1 week.

b) There are ☐ months in 1 year.

c) There are ☐ hours in 1 day.

d) There are ☐ days in March.

5   Here is a calendar for the month of June
    in 2020

JUNE

M	T	W	Th	F	Sa	Su
1	2	3	4	5	6	7
8	9	10	11	12	13	14
15	16	17	18	19	20	21
22	23	24	25	26	27	28
29	30					

a) How many days are in June?

b) On what day of the week was
    12 June 2020?

    _____

c) How many Saturdays were there in
    June in 2020?

d) Will June always have this many Saturdays? _____
    Explain your thinking.

    _____

6   Is Tiny's statement always true, sometimes true
    or never true? _____
    Explain your answer.

    There are 365
    days in a year.

    _____

7   Write <, > or = to compare the durations.

    a) 48 hours ◯ 3 days   c) 168 hours ◯ 1 week

    b) 30 months ◯ 3 years   d) 367 days ◯ 1 year

8   How many days are there in 54 weeks?

🔍 Crack the code

Use your answers in the coloured boxes to crack the code.

10	4	5	378	30	24	7
i	a	d	l	t	i	g

Can you explain
what the code
word means?

_____ _____ _____ _____ _____ _____ _____

105

Talk it out

List things you sometimes, never and always do in the morning (am) and in the afternoon (pm).

 In the morning, I sometimes …
I never … in the afternoon.

Share your lists with someone.

Can they share some of their own examples as well?

 Real world maths

What date is your birthday?

 You will need a 12-month calendar from this year.

In which month is it? _____

Is your birthday on a weekend this year? _____

What day is your birthday this year? _____

How many days are in your birthday month? ☐

How many days are there until your next birthday? ☐

How did you find these questions?

Time

Date:

Let's remember

1   How many days are there in 2 weeks?

2   Write the number 6 in Roman numerals. _____

3   Circle $\frac{1}{4}$ of the counters.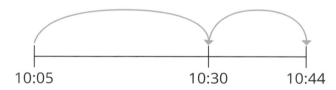

4   $20 \div 3 =$ [ ] remainder [ ]

Let's practise

1   Ron sets off on a walk at 10:05

He gets back at 10:44

How long was Ron's walk? [ ] minutes

Use the number line to help you.

10:05   10:30   10:44

2   Eva gets to the pool at 14:50

She leaves at 15:49

How many minutes did Eva stay at the pool? [ ] minutes

3   A TV show starts at 15:15 and lasts for 28 minutes.

Write the time the TV show ends as a digital time. [:]

4   The first clock shows the time Whitney starts playing in her garden.

She spends 45 minutes playing in the garden.

 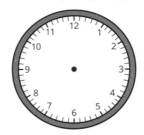

Draw hands on the second clock to show the time when Whitney finishes playing in the garden.

5   Complete the sentences.

a) There are ⬜ seconds in 1 minute.

b) There are ⬜ seconds in 2 minutes.

c) There are ⬜ seconds in 10 minutes.

6   Complete the statements.

a) 1 minute and 12 seconds = ⬜ seconds

b) 4 minutes and 38 seconds = ⬜ seconds

c) 205 seconds = ⬜ minutes and ⬜ seconds

7   Mo and Teddy both run a race.

Who was faster? Explain your answer.

_____

_____

My time was 354 seconds Mo

I ran the race in 3 minutes and 54 seconds. Teddy

Crack the code

Use your answers in the coloured boxes to crack the code.

Can you use the code word in a sentence?

600	59	25	14	278	6	60
n	c	s	s	d	e	o

_____ _____ _____ _____ _____ _____ _____

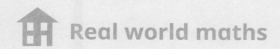 **Real world maths**

Write a list of the main things you did today.

Write the time you started and finished each thing. (You can guess if you don't know!)

 A schedule is a plan for your time.

Use the start and finish times to work out how long you spent doing each thing.

My schedule

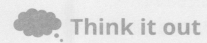 **Think it out**

The world has lots of different time zones.

Research the different time zones.

How many can you find?

What time will it be in New York when it is 6 pm in England?

_____

What time will it be in Dubai when it is 7 am in England?

_____

What time will it be in Pakistan when it is 11 am in England?

_____

How did you find these questions?

Block 4 Shape

In this block, we explore different **angles**. Remember, an **acute** angle is less than 90 **degrees**, a **right** angle is exactly 90 degrees and an **obtuse** angle is greater than 90 degrees.

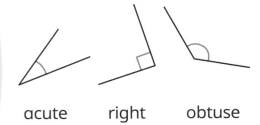

acute   right   obtuse

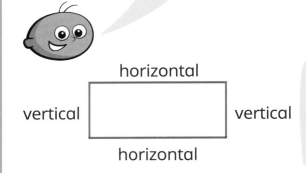

We identify **horizontal** and **vertical** lines in different shapes.
I've drawn a rectangle with two horizontal sides and two vertical sides.

parallel   perpendicular

We also draw **parallel** and **perpendicular** lines. Remember that parallel lines will never meet!

We identify **properties** of **3-D shapes**. My shape has 5 **vertices** and 5 **faces**. It is a square-based pyramid!

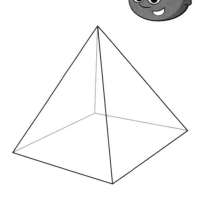

Here are some maths words that you'll see. Can you remember what they mean?

angle   acute   right angle   obtuse   horizontal   vertical
perpendicular   parallel   vertex/vertices   face   property   2-D/3-D

Shape

Date:

Let's remember

1   There are [   ] seconds in 3 minutes.

2   How many days are there in November? [   ]

3   What is £10 subtract £4 and 27p? £[   ] and [   ] p

4   What is 309 more than 587? [   ]

Let's practise

1   Here is a compass.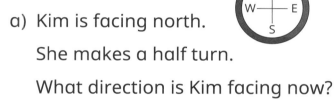

    a) Kim is facing north.

        She makes a half turn.

        What direction is Kim facing now?

        _____

> Think about the direction the hands on a clock turn to help you with clockwise and anti-clockwise.

    b) Teddy is facing west.

        Where is Teddy facing after a quarter turn clockwise? _____

    c) Tiny is facing south.

        Where is Tiny facing after a three-quarter turn

        anti-clockwise? _____

2   Mark the right angles on these triangles with a ⌐.

  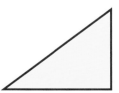

3   Ron is facing north. He turns clockwise until he is facing west.

    How many right angles does Ron turn through? [   ]

4   a) How many right angles does a square have?

   b) Write the name of another shape with the
       same number of right angles as a square. _____

5   Label the angles using the words. | acute | | obtuse | | right |

_____   _____   _____

6   Write < or > to compare the angles.

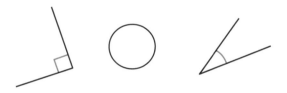

7   Draw a 2-D shape with two horizontal sides
    that are 50 mm long, two vertical sides
    that are 2 cm long, and at least one right angle.

> I am going to
> use the corner of
> my ruler to make
> sure I have made
> a perfect
> right angle.

Crack the code

Use your answers in the coloured boxes to crack the code.

896	4	180	3
u	n	t	r

____ ____ ____ ____

> Can you use
> the code word in
> a sentence?

 **Think it out**

The time is 20 minutes to 12

What time will it be when the minute hand has turned through 15 quarter turns clockwise?

_____

Can you draw the new time?

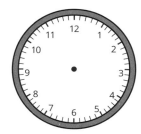

 Real world maths

Angles are everywhere!

Take a good look around your home.

Can you find some examples of right angles, acute angles and obtuse angles?

Which type of angle was the easiest to find?

Which was the hardest?

How did you find these questions?

Shape

Date:

Let's remember

1   Draw a horizontal line that is 4 cm long.

2   A film starts at 9:25 am. It lasts for 120 minutes.

     What time does the film finish? _____

3   521 pence = £ ☐ and ☐ p

4   893 has ☐ hundreds, ☐ tens and ☐ ones

Let's practise

1   a) Draw a pair of parallel lines.   b) Draw a pair of perpendicular lines.

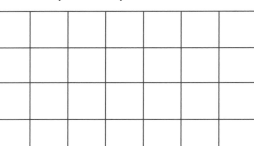   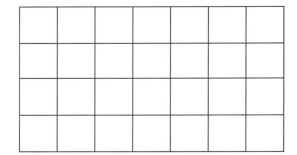

2   Is Tiny's statement always true, sometimes true or never true?

     _____

Parallel lines are horizontal lines that never meet.

     Explain your answer.

     _____

     _____

3 Complete the sentences.

   a) A triangle has ⬜ sides.

   c) A _____ has 6 sides.

   b) A pentagon has ⬜ sides.

   d) A quadrilateral has ⬜ sides.

4 Tick all the trapeziums.

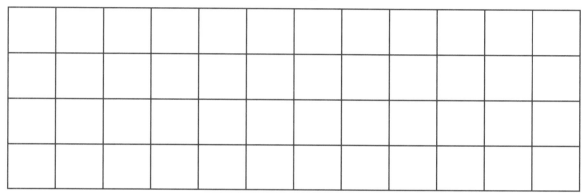

5 Draw 2 different hexagons on the grid.

6 Annie and Eva are describing 3-D shapes.

   Which shapes are they describing?

   My shape has a circular bottom and a pointy top.

   My shape has 8 vertices and 6 faces, equal in size.

   Annie: _____   Eva: _____

🔍 Crack the code

Use your answers in the coloured boxes to crack the code.

21	3	4	9
s	d	e	i

Can you use the code word in a sentence?

_____ _____ _____ _____

Real world maths

Use items from around your home to create your own set of 3-D shapes!

For example, you could make them from straws and marshmallows or sticks and sticky tack. You might even think of something better!

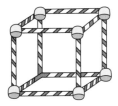

How many 3-D shapes can you make?

Were some harder to make than others? Why?

 ## Talk it out

You will find many 3-D shapes in your home.

Try to find something the shape of a:

- cuboid

- cylinder

- sphere

Explain to someone else how you can tell which shape they are.

 I can tell this is a ... because ...

How did you find these questions?

In this block, we explore different ways of presenting **data**.

We look at data that has been collected as **tallies**.
The **tally marks** in this table show how many cars of each colour passed the school in one hour.

Car colour	Silver	Black	Red	Blue
Number	ɪɪɪɪ ɪɪɪɪ ɪɪɪɪ ɪɪɪɪ ɪ	ɪɪɪɪ ɪɪɪɪ ɪɪɪɪ ɪɪ	ɪɪɪɪ ɪɪɪ	ɪɪɪɪ ɪɪɪɪ ɪ

Day	Sandwiches sold
Monday	●●●
Tuesday	●●●●
Wednesday	●●●
Thursday	●●●●●
Friday	●●●●●●●●●●

We use **pictograms** to represent data. This is a chart that uses pictures to show the data clearly. This one shows how many sandwiches are sold on different days.

Key: ● = 10 sandwiches

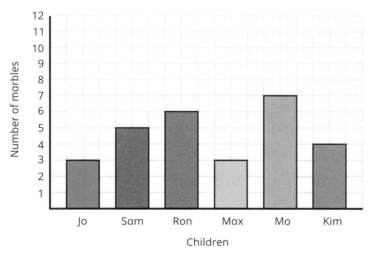

Bar charts are another clear way to represent data.

This one shows how many marbles each child has.

Here are some maths words that you'll see.

Can you remember what they mean?

data   table   tally chart   pictogram   bar chart

axes   labels   key   total

Statistics

Date:

Let's remember

1   A ball is what 3-D shape? _____

2   A 5-sided shape is called a _____.

3   420 seconds is equal to ☐ minutes.

4   8 × ☐ = 96

Let's practise

1   The pictogram shows the number of sandwiches sold each day at a sandwich shop.

Day	Sandwiches sold
Monday	●●●
Tuesday	●●●●
Wednesday	●●●
Thursday	●●●●●
Friday	●●●●●●●●

Key: ● = 10 sandwiches

a) On which day did they sell the most sandwiches? _____

b) On which days did they sell the same number of sandwiches?

_____ and _____

c) How many sandwiches did they sell on Thursday? ☐

d) How many fewer sandwiches did they sell on Monday

than Tuesday? ☐

e) How many sandwiches did they sell in total across

the week? ☐

2   The table shows the number of each type of berry in a bowl.

Fruit	Blackberries	Strawberries	Blueberries	Raspberries
Number	15	5	20	10

Display the results in the pictogram.

Fruit	Number of berries
Blackberries	
Strawberries	
Blueberries	
Raspberries	

Key: ⬤ = 2 berries

3   The bar chart shows the number of children in each year group at a school.

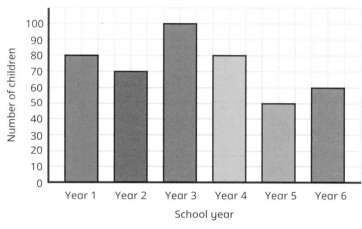

a) Which year group has the most children?

_____

b) Which year group has the fewest children?

_____

c) How many children are there in Year 1? ☐

d) How many more children are in Year 4 than Year 6? ☐

e) How many fewer children are in Year 2 than Year 3? ☐

f) How many children are in Years 1 and 2 in total? ☐

🔍 **Crack the code**

Use your answers in the coloured boxes to crack the code.

30	50	80	7	12	10
s	b	l	l	a	e

Can you use the code word in a sentence?

_____ _____ _____ _____ _____ _____

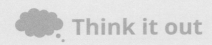 **Think it out**

A class of 30 children voted for their favourite animal.

- $\frac{3}{5}$ of the children voted for turtles.

- Half of the remaining children voted for dogs.

- 3 fewer children voted for cats than dogs.

- The rest of the children voted for giraffes.

Draw a pictogram to represent the information.

Animal	Number of children
Turtles	
Dogs	
Cats	
Giraffes	

Key:

How did you find these questions?

Statistics

Date:

Let's remember

1   A key on a pictogram shows that 1 square = 5 children.
How many squares are needed to represent 45 children?

2   What is the mathematical name for this 3-D shape?

_____

3   How many right angles are in half a turn?

4   507 – 30 =

Let's practise

1   Here are some shapes.

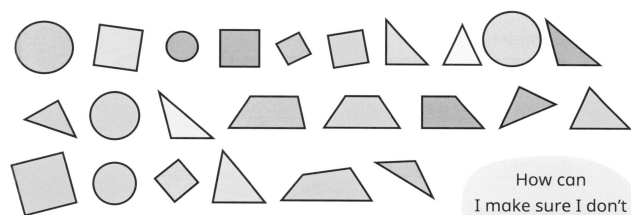

Complete the tally chart to show how many of
each shape you can count.

How can
I make sure I don't
miss any?

Shape	Tally	Total
Square		
Triangle		
Trapezium		
Circle		

2 The table shows the number of stickers children got in a week at school.

Child	Jo	Sam	Ron	Max	Mo	Kim
Stickers	3	5	9	4	7	8

Use the information in the table to complete the bar chart.

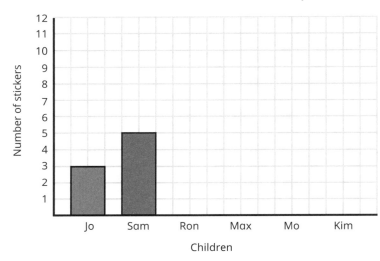

3 100 children take part in after-school sports.

a) Complete the table.

	Hockey	Football	Rounders	Total
Girls	14	25	10	
Boys	20	21	10	
Total				100

b) How many girls play football?

c) How many boys take part in total?

d) Which sport do the same number of girls and boys play? _____

e) How many more girls play football than hockey?

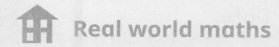 **Real world maths**

Think about the different colours of cars.

Which colour do you think you see most often? _____

Which colour do you think you see least often? _____

With an adult, stand on the pavement near where you live for 10 or 15 minutes. Make a tally of the different colours of car that pass you.

Were your predictions correct? _____

How many different colours did you record? _____

I will draw a bar chart to show my results.

How did you find these questions?   :(

123

Consolidation

Date:

Let's remember

1. What number does this represent? 卌 卌Ⅰ ☐

2. How many vertices does a sphere have? ☐

3. Which month is the 4ᵗʰ month of the year? _____

4. $\frac{1}{3} + \frac{1}{3} = \frac{\boxed{}}{\boxed{}}$

Let's practise

1. Work out the perimeter of each shape.

a)
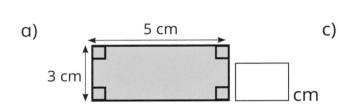
5 cm
3 cm
☐ cm

b)
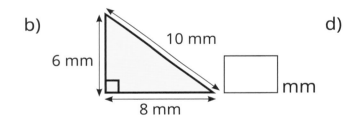
10 mm
6 mm
8 mm
☐ mm

c)
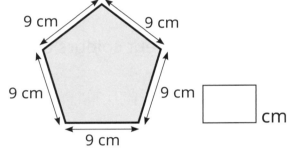
9 cm   9 cm
9 cm   9 cm
9 cm
☐ cm

d)
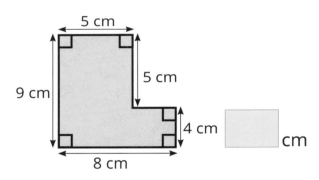
5 cm
5 cm
9 cm
4 cm
8 cm
☐ cm

2. Complete the calculations.

a) $\frac{2}{11} + \frac{5}{11} = \frac{\boxed{}}{\boxed{}}$

b) $\frac{7}{8} = \frac{\boxed{}}{\boxed{}} + \frac{3}{8}$

c) $\frac{9}{14} - \frac{3}{14} = \frac{\boxed{}}{\boxed{}}$

d) $1 - \frac{3}{4} = \frac{\boxed{}}{\boxed{}}$

3. Complete the multiplications.

a) 3 × 16 = ☐   c) 34 × 3 = ☐

b) 5 × 26 = ☐   d) 17 × 5 = ☐

4. Complete the divisions.

a) 68 ÷ 2 = ☐   b) 90 ÷ 5 = ☐   c) 81 ÷ 3 = ☐

5 Complete the divisions.

a) $17 \div 4 = \boxed{}$ remainder $\boxed{}$ c) $48 \div 5 = \boxed{}$ remainder $\boxed{}$

b) $50 \div 3 = \boxed{}$ remainder $\boxed{}$ d) $100 \div 3 = \boxed{}$ remainder $\boxed{}$

6 Draw a 4 cm horizontal line in the space below.

Draw a 6 cm parallel line 3 cm
above the 4 cm line.

Join the ends of each line together
to make a quadrilateral.

Which quadrilateral have you drawn? _____

7 Sam wants to post both of these presents.

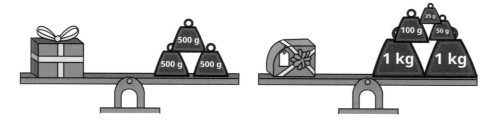

Use the table to work out how much it will cost to post both presents.

Parcel size	Weight	Postage
Small	Less than 1 kg	£2 and 63p
Medium	1 kg to 2 kg	£3 and 21p
Large	More than 2 kg	£4 and 65p

It will cost £ $\boxed{}$ and $\boxed{}$ p

🔍 Crack the code

Use your answers in the coloured boxes to crack the code.

85	0	33	27	31	1	130	2	4
g	p	m	r	c	a	o	i	t

Explain what the code word means.

_____ _____ _____ _____   _____ _____ _____   _____ _____

125

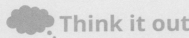 **Think it out**

A pentomino is a shape made up of 5 squares.

Here is an example.

There are 12 pentominoes in total.

Can you draw the other 11?

 Talk it out

Take some time to have a look back through your book.

Which maths topics did you enjoy the most?

Which did you find the most difficult?

Create a poster of the things you found the most difficult.

Include pictures and instructions to help you remember.

> I enjoyed … because …
> I found … the most difficult because …

How did you find these questions?

Summer term   Self-assessment
Time to reflect

 Look back through the work you have done this term. Think about what you enjoyed and what you found easy or hard. Talk about this to your teacher or someone at home.

 Look back at the telling the time questions on page 104. Write the time "ten past four" on the analogue and digital clocks below.

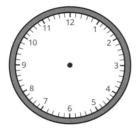   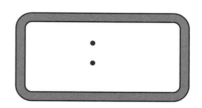

I am more confident with telling the time on _____

because _____.

or ☐ I am confident with telling the time on both analogue and digital clocks.

 What type of angles are these? Draw lines to join each angle to the correct word.

acute   obtuse   right

 Circle one of the statements to show how that made you feel.

| I am confident and could teach someone else. | I think I understand but I need more practice. | I don't understand and need help. |

127

Look back at the bar charts in Block 5.
Who has the most marbles, according to the bar chart below?

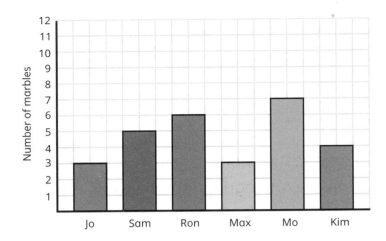

_____ has the most marbles.

Colour the face that shows how you felt when answering the question.

I get it!   I need a little help.   I don't get it.

Have a think about all the work you've done this term.
What went well?
What do you still need to practise?

I am confident with _____

_____

_____

I will practise _____

_____

_____